O B A M A
TEA PARTIES
&
G O D
of

Providence, Patriotism and Faith

LISAServes, LLC
1800 Lavaca Street
Suite 109
Austin, TX 78701
www.lisafritsch.com

LISAServes books may purchase for educational, business, or sales promotional use. For information please write: lisa@lisaserves.com

Second edition publishing

1. Religion. 2. Politics and Government. 3. Ethics 4. God. 5. African-American authors. 6.Lisa Fritsch

Dedicated to the loves of my life

Our Father
Michael, my heart
Bowie, my soul
Elenor, my spirit
My Mom

C O R A M   D E O

CONTENTS

FOREWORD
The Gospel

When the Pharisees questioned, "Teacher, which is the first and greatest commandment in the law of Moses?"

Jesus replied, "You must love the LORD your God with all your heart, all your soul, and all your mind. This is the first and the greatest commandment. A second is equally important: 'Love your neighbor as yourself.' The entire law and all the demands of the prophets are based on these two commandments."

Then Jesus said to the crowds and to his disciples, "The teachers of religious law and the Pharisees are the official interpreters of the law of Moses. So practice and obey whatever they tell you, but don't follow their example. For they don't practice what they teach. They crush people with unbearable religious demands and never lift a finger to ease the burden.

Don't let anyone call you 'Rabbi' for you have only one teacher, and all of you are equal as brothers and sisters. And don't address anyone here on Earth as 'Father,' for only God in heaven is your spiritual Father. And don't let anyone call you 'Teacher,' for you have only one teacher, the Messiah. The greatest among you must be a servant. But those who exalt themselves will be humbled, and those who humble themselves will be exalted.

I am the vine, you are the branches; he who abides in Me and I in him, he bears much fruit, for apart from Me you can do nothing.

Matthew 22:37-40; 45-47:1-4; 5-12 John 15:5

Obama, Tea Parties, and GOD

of Providence, Patriotism, and Faith

OBAMA REVISED INTRO-APOLOGY

I began writing this book in January 2010, fresh off my second appearance on Glenn Beck, knee deep in the Tea Party movement, speaking across the country, making television appearances and being approached left and right for political consulting.

At once, the career I'd worked long and hard for was taking shape while my arrogance and assuredness in conservatism and right wing politics was becoming a full blown idolatry common in most ideologues. I am deeply bereaved at my idolatry of conservative values as the solution for humanity. After all, we are saved by grace, not conservative values, or anything else.

It wasn't until I took a leap of faith to come from behind the microphone and the black box of television that I immersed myself in the midst of what I'd been ranting about for more than a decade. I'd finally decided I'd had enough of talking and criticizing behind the scenes. I would step into the arena to be the change I wanted to see in my party and politics.

Running in the Republican Primary for Governor of Texas, I became painfully aware of my ignorance and the truth surrounding my "fight the good fight" rants.

My ebook, *Politically Corrected* is a manifesto on those corrections and I will let those reflections stand alone.

I'd considered shelving *Obama Tea Parties and God* until I realized much of the content still offers truth and strong opportunity for transformation on the left and right. Too, there is a certain necessity and humility in facing up in hindsight.

I could not relaunch the book revised and revisited without expressing the regret in my heart of my early antagonism of President Barack Obama and the First Lady.

Among the strongest of my corrections was that my animosity and opinions about his election and intentions were justified. They were not. I allowed my narrow vision and broad acceptance of all things on the right, blind me to what I couldn't possibly know and prevent me from seeing or understanding any good his tenure could bring.

For my misguided and willful pride, I will forever be disappointed in myself. I have no reason to expect that the president or Mrs. Obama will ever read these words or this book, but that won't prevent me from expressing deep apology and remorse for adding to the heap of ill-will awaiting he and his family as they became the first African-American family to call the White House home.

Behaving and speaking as a true believer in Christ would have found me loving them as I love myself, wishing them well, and accepting their leadership as the chosen will of God. I can say with all sincerity and humility, I love you Mr. President. I wish you and the beautiful First Family family all the very best today and for all time.

For the reader, I hope and pray the same for you and yours.

Love,
Lisa

SECTION I
Obama

PROVIDENCE

Kool-aid Kids

If Obama duped us, then we really are stupid, so that cannot be. Could it go something more like this? We were after something. Americans sold out. And, we had sold out a long time before Obama came along. Americans gave up a lot to build that pedestal that Obama stood on. We set him up in such a way that he could only fall, and we could only be disappointed. What transpired in Obama becoming our 44th President is a fascinating look at who we were and where we are headed as a nation.

Our "wanna get away" attitude wasn't surprising. September 11th emotionally drained us. Hurricane Katrina profoundly disappointed us. The war in Iraq and Afghanistan frightened us. And after eight years of George W. Bush, we were all done with drama. So, when Obama rode in on his high horse of hope and change, we all wanted a ride. The fact that Barack Obama was a junior senator with no prior political or professional experience outside of being a community organizer - the equivalent to an internship with the Red Cross – should have made us laugh, but instead we found it refreshing. Part of the change, I guess. In Hillary Clinton's experience and political legacy we found fault with her as the establishment candidate, while embellishing Obama as modern and visionary. And, instead of getting an 'F' for the hazard of inexperience, we eagerly passed Obama on rhetoric, poise and most of all, guilt.

America decided. The mainstream media decided. Very few of our minds could be changed. Though it became clear to many of us that something was amiss, even all wrong, it would be too late to reverse the damage that drinking the Kool-aid had done. Those who protested perhaps did so too loudly. And, those who would be forever enamored were convicted in armor so dense that our nation once knit together in Obama, forged a divide much greater because of him.

We all had a role to play: Obama, the media, ourselves. Americans generally would say a guy they would like to have a beer with. Still, it takes more than charisma to turn speeches into a viable political campaign pummeling rivals who had experience, military service, political legacy, and money on their side (or so it seemed). He simply couldn't have done it without our help. So let's begin with –as the solving of all problems do – with ourselves.

CHAPTER ONE

Ourselves

'Take up your cross' 'My yoke is easy and my burden light"

Matthew 10:24; 11:28

"We can do this the easy way, or, the hard way," my mom often said to me after I'd been caught in one of my latest shenanigans. It wasn't long before I discovered the best way to avoid the 'hard' way was to take what I now know as the hard, easy route in the first place. C.S. Lewis, author of *Mere Christianity* writes, "Teachers will tell you that it is the laziest boy in the class who works the hardest in the end. Laziness means more work in the long run. Or, look at it this way. In a battle, or in mountain climbing, there is often one thing which it takes a lot of pluck to do; but it is also, in the long run, the safest thing to do. If you funk it, you will find yourself, hours later, in far worse danger. The cowardly thing is also the most dangerous thing." It is the same in our daily and political lives. The hard, easy is the route no one wants to trek. It is the long-suffering route of discipline and the carrying of the heavy load up front. The reward comes only after all this is put in. For a while now, Americans have been looking for the quick, easy – and it seemed we might pull it off, almost.

Obama was our quick, easy way. In one vote we tried to heal the painful scars of our racist past, embrace the 21st century with fresh and youthful leadership, buy the world a coke and teach it how to sing. We should have known that no matter who we elected, it could have never been this easy.

We were ripe to fall for this empty hope and change nonsense at the time. Many of our reasons are understandable, nevertheless, must be addressed lest we make the same mistake again. Should we think we won't get fooled again, let's understand ourselves better.

We Were Tired

We'd earned our weariness. In the last ten years, we'd been through an emotional hell. September 11, 2001 dealt an ugly blow to our nation's sovereignty. Two years later we were fighting the war on terror. In 2005 Hurricane Katrina opened our eyes to the depths of poverty in New Orleans' predominantly black community. Americans watched as too many poor, black, Americans huddled in a packed football stadium just waiting. The horrific images of those stranded on freeways without transportation or a clue of how to respond to the devastation ripped through our television sets shocking us, disgusting us, and angering us. Economic worry grew as 2008 brought a rising unemployment level of 6.1 percent (though wouldn't we like to see that number again). And, finally we were losing young men and women every day in Iraq and Afghanistan. The war and death toll especially was a drain on us financially and emotionally. We wanted to fight the war on terror, but it was taking too long. Many of us wanted out.

Barack Obama promised to fix all of these things, with a new tone, a change. Thank goodness, we thought. He promised to bring our sons and daughters home from war, have the world smile on us, and bring America to post racial unity and equality. A fine chap, we reckoned. What we never considered is what that truly meant to be in his cup. In ours!

Democrats were of course thrilled at this new, "clean and well-spoken" – in Joe Biden's words – presidential

13

candidate. Republicans suddenly became "Independents" in order to ride the wave of Obama's style and popularity. He was so catastrophically perfect, who would ruin the façade and the hopes and dreams of a country with questions. Besides we were tired. We had been fighting the last eight years already. We didn't have the energy to fight perfection.

Because we were hungry for a new beginning, Obama's promise – turned lecture - of hope and change sounded good. What we hadn't realized, is that we'd supplied our own hefty doses of hope and change in the face of tragedy.

After the attacks in 2001, the country huddled together in love and reverence for who we are, but quickly became unglued at the thought of actually fighting for it. Those few days, weeks, and months of unity stemming from tragedy is what we missed. Obama gave us that feeling again. We could all agree his star was bright. We concurred his speeches sounded good. What we never stopped to consider was that we were bright and *we* were good. We were worthy because of who we are and had been, not because of who he professed to make us become. Had we been more alert to our own star rising, our fascination with Obama's wouldn't have been so obsessive.

It should be said that we felt unity and love in those tender days following September 11 because of one another. No one person made us feel this way. We prayed. We did the work. We extended ourselves to each other. We put our own lives aside. We called our neighbors to make sure they were safe. We took in friends and families from New York who would be homeless or too traumatized after the attack. We befriended new neighbors who moved from New York. We energized ourselves and gave ourselves new hope. Despite how wonderfully Rudy Giuliani handled the cleanup and emotional aftermath of 9/11, or, how comforting President Bush's national address, the

American people and their spirit of humanity is what got us through that tragic moment. We prayed. We stepped up. We showed true patriotism for one another and our country.

Hurricane Katrina divided us along racial lines and like it, or not, we were forced to watch a media circus, that pondered among other ridiculous things, whether or not George Bush cared about black people. Despite what the media tried to tell us, we forged ahead in brotherhood. While there was media sensationalizing, pundit grandstanding, and uninspired leadership, ordinary Americans took action. Ordinary Americans took food to shelters and churches. Americans took in displaced families. Ordinary Americans took out their checkbooks and donated an extraordinary 1.3 billion dollars - at least- in corporate and foundation giving toward the rebuilding after Hurricane Katrina. We prayed. We stepped up. We loved one another.

Though by 2008 we were completely off our game and our resolve weakened. We'd forgotten much of what we'd endured over the last several years and perhaps we were eager to do so. A fresh start felt right. After eight years of Clinton, and eight years of Bush, we felt we had outgrown the necessity of proven leadership and solid experience in a political candidate. This was part of the new tone. That was Barack Obama. Barack Obama was popular with the young, college crowd – no great sin in that. Still, for the first time kids were telling their parents how to vote, an historical first. We were cashing in everything to support the clean, well spoken senator with nothing to back it up but good speeches. We traded our life experience for a special moment. We put aside the query needed in making sound decisions for supple rhetoric and naïve promises. We lost our integrity. All that was to be good about ourselves, we left to him. We decided that his goodness could be good enough for all of us. We were too tired and plain worn out to ask for anything more. He indeed became a political messiah. We told him so.

"Hacuna Matata"

One of my favorite scenes in the movie, *The Lion King,* is where young lion, Simba, remembers who he was born to be. Simba was deceived out of his rightful place as King and banished from his pride by Scar, a diabolical uncle and enemy of his own pride. Simba ends up living on a prairie out in the woods with a bunch of animals, that would normally be lunch, and has adapted to their 'hakuna matata' lifestyle. Hakuna Matata is a don't worry, be happy philosophy of life that is casual and free. Simba is content there until an old lion friend finds him during a hunt. She alerts him to the devastation Scar has caused. Simba is uneasy to return; after all, he isn't that regal lion anymore. Until, one day he gets a vision from his father encouraging him to, "remember who you are." Suddenly, hakuna matata is not good enough. His eyes are open and his commitment to his pride renewed.

What exactly does committing to America mean and how did we fail? I don't believe we failed, we simply forgot who we were. After Obama became President it was very clear who we were not.

Remembering who we are means America is going to have to grow up. That growing up is going to mean that we have to know exactly who we are and who we are not. What does it mean to be an American? What does that privilege entail and what do we do to protect it? Our country was not founded on many of the notions we have recently adopted. Until recently, too few of us have been willing to put the effort of understanding the true greatness of this country.

Getting to this greatness was the hard, easy. It took a great deal of courage, blood, and sacrifice. We already know this, but we've been so comfortable in our greatness, we started to take all of it for granted. We supplanted luxury for greatness. We turned the American dream into a fantasy land of adjustable rate mortgages, home flipping folly, blowout vacations, and bling, bling madness. When all along American greatness is much simpler and more sustainable than this. American greatness is built on the promise of opportunity, equality and protecting the sovereignty of the land. American greatness requires us to remember who we are.

We fell for the quick, easy with the smooth rhetoric and silver smile because our vanity made us complacent. We were vain and wise in our own eyes because we were so comfortable being comfortable. We were so focused on getting on to something new that we weren't watching what was happening under the Bush administration. While the bottom is falling out under Obama, the truth is that while we were sleeping under the roof of our adjustable rate mortgages, our house was already catching fire, but we were not paying attention. We were slowly burning for several years by 2008. Our national debt had been growing and social programs too for the last ten years. We were voting for American idols and reading about *Dancing with the Stars*. We were dazed and crazed in a zombie like WHEEL --- OF--- FORTUNE!!!! existence where everyone and everything looked fine, but inside this country's core was crumbling.

Americans were living in homes they couldn't afford, credit was being passed out like cheap church cookies, and we were seemingly living the good life. Everything that was fine was not. Why did all this go unnoticed? It wasn't only that we were watching *American Idol*, but mostly because we thought we deserved to be one. We felt entitled to a nice home, car, vacations, bonuses, and steady jobs. But we are not. Our overt vanity disillusioned us that we could betray hard work, delayed gratification, and sacrifice turning something for nothing into a value. In looking back on our history, we know this is not part of our founding philosophy.

This is one of the deepest betrayals we inflicted upon ourselves because it led us into one of the world's biggest lies: that we are less without material excess. This is not the American way. Americans were never so rich due to financial riches alone, but the promise of opportunity that made it possible. In the last few generations there has been a great and unprecedented effort to pit the haves against the have-nots. A movement to urge the Government to be accountable to the 'little guy' took hold. Obama saying that he "thinks it's better to spread the wealth around" is part of this. Wake up, dear friends, you are in America. There is no 'little' guy. The little guy is exactly why we became who we are. Still, there is an individual responsibility to that notion.

Government can never equalize material success. Our American founders realized long ago that this is exactly what was wrong with the aristocracy. It gave credence only to special persons and left ordinary people to serfdom and second class citizenry. America was tremendous in its founding because it held equality in the hands of our Creator and made the way for individuals, despite their heritage and genealogy to advance and have liberty. This opportunity isn't a guarantee of success and abundance. It is a promise of possibilities and the FREEDOM to choose one's life direction and purpose.

By the time Obama came onto the presidential scene in 2008, we had moved on from the lantern of hard work and sacrifice and onto the age of the quick, easy where shallow celebrity was commonplace and connecting with each other meant 'MySpace'. We were subsisting under the pretense of the American dream: a house, two cars, a chicken in every pot. No one was asking how the dream grew to a 4,000 square foot house for a construction worker making $30k a year, two BMW's, and lobster in the pot instead of a chicken.

Life was good, only it wasn't living. It was all magical thinking. We must remember that America was built to last. This pretense is not. That pretense is exactly what made Obama's divide and conquer strategy that much more successful. He would put our commitment to our country to the test by singling out the rich and the poor. He would size them up making greatness about tax brackets, race, social class, and political party instead of character, hard work, and integrity.

In our hearts, Americans know that we are not entitled to extremes of opulent success and luxury. We believe enough in ourselves and each other to know in our hearts that family, service, charity and humanity is real and lasting greatness. In our hearts, we know that our love for one another runs deep. We know in our hearts that we can be counted on when the going gets rough. We have done it, time and again. We've handed out this grace and love and we've thankfully received it. Think about it, can anyone really starve in this country? Do the poorest people in this country have a clue of what it is like to live in the best of the worst conditions of a third world country? The answer is no to both.

Commitment & Going the Distance.

Remembering who we are also means that we must make a firm commitment to the allegiance and promises we make to America. Obama was extremely successful masterful in divide and conquer. Because this election was about the changing of the haves and giving false hope to the "have-nots," our insecurity about our commitment made us vulnerable to the Robin Hood politics of "spreading the wealth" around. Obama held our past trespasses against us every chance he could, reminding us that he was for the "little" guy. He would put us down in the global press, remarking how ugly Americans had been a global bully, instead of a friend.

(As an aside to this point, "The New York Times" ran an op-ed in July 2010 from Desmond Tutu urging Obama to back up his $1 billion promise to spend at least as much as George W. Bush did to Aids in Africa.) He chose to be a citizen of the world and he expected Americans to be also. But many of us knew this was breaking a covenant with our beloved country. Scary as it is, many more did not see that he was seeking not only our approval in betraying our beloved country, but also our compliance. We started to believe in this.

We can compare our devotion to our country to that of a marriage. If a strong marriage is really to survive, the husband and wife must resolve that past wrongs and trespasses will not become a drum. Instead, they will carry the whole of their past – good, ugly, and bad – like a fertilizer into their future to make their marriage grow stronger. The pair will have to make a firm commitment to rely on what they love about one another to be enough. A marriage should not turn based on the season's current storms. This is little more than a pinky-swear. True commitment is only overturned by savagery, gross betrayal, or abuse. Otherwise, the grass will continually look greener. The loosely committed will eventually succumb to the temptation to do what is easier. Run!

In electing Obama we ran from our convictions and promises to America. And, if you think about it, wasn't it truly the only way we could justify his presidency? Obama reminded us what we loved and loathed about ourselves. The smooth part was that when he reminded us of what we loathed in ourselves, he redeemed us with himself. Electing him would be the first step in washing away the sins, and righting the ship with change. Where he approved of us we were great, and electing him was the hope. When

20

he dismissed us, we were low and unworthy, but redeemed with him as the symbol of change. Therefore, we started to focus greatly on the change aspect of his leadership instead of moving forward in the foundation of what we loved about ourselves and this nation, from whence true hope flows.

Obama did have the charisma that helped make the fleeing easier, but it was our country's inner demons that made us run. Like the temptress in the red dress, the younger secretary at the office, or the slick shyster in the suit, Obama was no change at all from the status quo. Like the other woman who offers nothing different from a husband's wife except that she is new and untested, or, the shyster who can offer the wife nothing greater than her current husband, Obama was a distraction from the hard work it would take to get our commitment back on track. What of the hope and change? The adulterer hopes are pinned only on the idea of starting over. The adulteress hopes the change will mean better flatware and nicer handbags, with hopefully as little change required of her as possible. Americans were the adulterer in our relationship with America and our values because we ran away from who we are. We drank the wrong cup.

We Wanted Redemption: Our Guilt

Americans still feel a great deal of shame in our past. While we have had many social triumphs as a nation: World War I, World War II, The Civil Rights Movement, our charity and commitment to Africa and other third world nations, this young nation still agonizes over the stain of slavery and its lingering effects of discrimination and distrust. We are desperate for redemption of slavery's past however we can get it: affirmative action, quotas, political correctness, we will take it.

Part of falling in love so deeply with Barack Obama had very little to do with his charm, but more so to do with our wanting to be like him. When in 2004 a young, beautiful black man professed America's greatness and confessed that 'no other country on Earth is my story even possible," we felt vindicated. We thought collectively our moment arrived. We would be spared the agony of debate, discussion, and the acknowledgement of race. The plan was simple: If our President is post-racial; America would be also.

We'd found a moderate man who understood us. He was all of us and none of us: black, white, foreign, exotic, and with just that right touch of down to earth charm (hoops anyone?) to keep us from getting nervous uncomfortable. He was from Hawaii – an American respite away from the dogged history of the South and the uppity, stiff reputation of the North. He was so different from anyone else we'd ever known, and he loved us. We loved him back.

We Wanted our Moment

We would soon find out the hard way, that this love wasn't cheap. We would feel duped, scammed, cornered, and frankly dirty as he kicked off a campaign in which he increasingly zinged us as greedy, global bullies run amok. American was a cesspool of elite, racists who take every opportunity to sock it to the little guy. We were betrayed to find out that he spent 20 years in a church listening to hate speech about our beloved country where his pastor, Jeremiah Wright was caught on film saying, "God damn America" and calling Hillary Clinton a racist. Many of us woke up then, but still some of us wanted to remain in the matrix of denial. If you are like me, you were surprised when all of this came to the surface; you still had many friends with shared values who still planned on voting for Barack Obama. Wasn't it odd, how the room became so quiet?

In my first appearance on "Glenn Beck" in 2009, the first question to the panel and audience of black conservatives was, "how many of you voted for Obama?" I was shocked to see so many hands raised. I wasn't able to filter my initial thoughts and blurted out, "What? How could this be happening?"

I was astounded to be around like-minded brethren who would still vote for Barack Obama after so much proof that his philosophy was counter to our conservative principles. I wasn't the lone conservative on a panel of liberals; we were supposed to be conservatives for goodness sakes!!! Some said they voted because they believed in the change. Some leveled with the truth: that they copped to the historical moment of voting for the first black President. I did feel duped then, really. Was I naïve to think that the purpose of realizing the dream was the individual liberty to accept and reject a person based on character alone? How can we truly move forward on the content of our character if conservatives, blacks, women, are afraid to reject someone because they have uncontrollable genetic attributes in common? Isn't our country's sovereignty too important to leave to the equivalent of flipping a coin?

This and other intimate revelations convinced me that America hadn't been duped. We had ignored our gut. We ignored our voice. We ignored ourselves, our principles, and our country in order to support a moment. A moment that people decided to make possible at all costs. America needed to have the dream of the black president come true. Never mind he isn't traditionally black in the way of Black history. He is black in the same way that Mariah Carey's voice gives her enough cross over credence to make her acceptable to the black community. "Sounding like that, she might as well be black."

We so wanted and needed a moment where people THOUGHT we were perfect - that we had figured the whole racism and discrimination thing out. Blacks wanted to redeem the history of blacks as being less than in our country and prove that Dr. King's dream could really come true. Whites wanted to prove with a dot of a ballot pen that they had washed all their prejudices away. America was voting for that one moment, where we could buy, or elect our way into redemption without having to really lift a finger ourselves. Unfortunately, we were betrayed by our own hands, not exclusively those of the media, or Barack Obama.

The buyer's remorse we so often here about in electing Obama is little more than good old fashioned guilt. Acting out of guilt is often the quick, easy way to cover up a problem that really takes dedicated effort and longevity of hand to remedy. Like the guilty husband who shows up spontaneously with flowers to the unsuspecting wife, or the weekend dad who allows the kids all the ice cream they can hold to compensate for his daily absence, or the parent who buys the latest toys, but won't spend time, guilty fixes always come up short.

Guilt isn't always a terrible thing. Guilt usually stems from love. In the proper context, guilt serves a noble purpose in making us realize we ought to be better than we have been. We must remember that the harder thing to do is usually the right thing to do.

My mother became a single parent after she and my father divorced. I was in first grade and our lives were turned upside down. I would be different from most children in my neighborhood not only because I was an only child, but also in having only one parent. I didn't fully realize the burdens my mother faced until I became a mother myself. She was also a loner. Ironically, that they ostracized her strengthened and convicted her. Sometimes the strong stand alone. It would have been easier to remarry, the idea of a stepfather or an extended family unnerved her. She could have saved her back and a couple extra dollars a month and rented an apartment. Yet, she was steadfast in her belief and faith that God made a way for her to provide a home for her child and that he would help her keep it if she did her part. She could have taken Government assistance, but she would not compromise her principles and have us live beneath them. And so she soldiered on determined and struggling most of the way.

I knew we didn't have a lot, but like most kids I still wanted nice clothes and the latest toys. We couldn't afford it. My mother worked two, sometimes three, jobs (depending on the timeline) just to put food on the table, send me to piano, and enroll me in dance classes. That is what I got and there was little left after this. I wore Lee jeans, not Guess. I had white tabbed sneakers, not shiny blue Keds.

Imagine the turbulence of my envy when one of my dear classmates, who was in the same predicament of divorced parents, would show up in fancy dresses, or, holding the very cabbage patch doll I could never get. Her mother worked an extra job to make sure she and her sister fit in. Her mother took Government assistance for the food and used the extra money to buy what they wanted, not just what they needed. The guilt her mom felt for being a single parent (their father would never visit, or return) led her to extreme cases of overcompensation. She channeled most of her efforts into making sure they had all the appearances of a two parent family. She rented nice homes, drove a good car, had fancy furniture, and the kids had all the clothes, Little Debbie snack cakes, and video games to boot. In my house, a box of popsicles for a good report card was considered the jackpot. We drove the Vega until the wheels came off and a little Mazda hatchback until it literally kicked *us* to the curb.

Unfortunately for my classmate's mom all that guilt-ridden, material compensation never paid off. My classmate and her sister were bad as Hell: refusing to study, destroying toys as quickly as they got them, cursing teachers, and starting fights at school. Somehow, they never measured up to all the things lavished on them.

My mother channeled her guilt differently. Although she was often criticized for the hard line she took. Plenty of my aunts, my grandparents, and her friends took pity on me on many occasions. Still, Debra knew that she had to take the hard, easy way to make sure that I could get on in the world. Having nice clothes, the cutest backpack, and the latest doll wouldn't cut it. Even as a child, I knew that my mother was showing character and faith in us. Most importantly, she was showing faith in God. She knew if she did her part, that HE would do His. *"Take up your Cross. My yoke is easy and my burden light."* She wasn't hoping or living for the adoration of those around us. She wasn't seeking the approval of the outside world. She honored the commitment to who we were in taking the hard, easy.

Needless to say, the lavish spending was a waste in the end for my classmates. The same is true of the guilty purchase America made in electing Barack Obama. It left us resentful and awkward in our resentment. The worst part is that not only did we lose respect for him but also for ourselves.

We are not so angry with Obama. We had ourselves to blame. We lost more respect for ourselves than Obama. This loss of self-respect is hard to shake. Because as much as we built this pedestal Obama has been standing on, we are now forced to take it down. This is much harder to do and makes our guilt that much worse. In taking it down, we are forced to acknowledge why we put it up in the first place and to defend our reason for taking it down. Some of us would rather leave the pedestal in place than to acknowledge our guilt. More than this, it takes us back to the spot we were trying to avoid in the first place. He's black. And, that's part of the guilt.

Our guilt is understandable. Our country's slave legacy is a terrible stain that we should never forget, but part of lessening the hurt is to deal with the guilt correctly. We've tried so many ways at the quick, easy: quotas, affirmative action, political correctness, and now our affirmative action President. Still, the past hovers. We've made great progress, but it never seems to be enough for those who continually feel shortchanged. Why?

At the heart of rectifying guilt with the quick, easy is condescension. Favors, praise, and pay-offs done with guilty hands is the ultimate backhanded 6th place trophy. Where the guilty hand gives false credit, it takes away truth's light and the splendor of possibilities that might have been. Underneath the veil of guilty smiles, is fear and self loathing. The quick, easy gives us that fleeting moment of joy and happiness, but just as soon denies us peace. Guilty pay-offs never fully antes up the goods. The inaugural day of our 44th President was a beautiful, glowing occasion where we indeed got our moment, but that is long gone and forgotten. We've made a left turn back to guilt's woe and dropped off from whence we started, if not further behind.

ADDENDUM

Our humanity and our capacity to love one another is all we have. We don't have a greed problem, vanity problem, an Obama problem, a patriotism problem. Our only problem is in our inability to put love first. If we have riches beyond the depths of the ocean but no love, we have nothing. If we have the mightiest army, but lack love, we are weak. If we have every opportunity to succeed and thrive, but we don't have love, we won't have peace.

True equality and racial reconciliation lies in our willingness to love one another as we love ourselves and to love the Lord God with all our hearts, putting our faith and trust wholeheartedly in his power, not a president no matter left, right, or in between.

When our hearts are right, our love boundless, and our hearts and minds fixed on the will and power of God, who the President is won't matter. The color of our skin will simply be shades of his glory.

CHAPTER TWO

The Media Mix

"I have to tell you, you know, it's part of reporting this case, this election, the feeling most people get when they hear Barack Obama's speech. My, I felt this thrill going up my leg."

Chris Matthews, MSNBC journalist

THE LOVERS
The Media (CNN, ABC, CBS, MSNBC)

From the beginning, there was a frenzied sense of urgency that should have made many of us leery. Nearly all coverage centered on the Presidential campaign of Barack Obama. He was as overexposed then as he is now. Once elected, the sense of urgency continued as *TIME* magazine would make President Obama its "Person of the Year" with the headline of "Why History Can't Wait." Many of us were on the same page with the media in 2006. We loved Obama's story and thought his inexperience could be overcome by his moderate style of leadership. The media took great pains to re-convince us of what many were already convinced: Obama was the one. With effusive dedication and focus, the media aligned themselves in Obama's corner throwing journalistic integrity out of the window.

Once the media got their election victory, their spin cycle kept running. The "thrill went up my leg" Chris Matthews of MSNBC is a good example. The "Hardball" host appeared on 'Morning Joe" with Joe Scarborough announcing, I want to do everything I can do to make this thing work, the new presidency work." At least Joe Scarborough reminded Matthews that he was a journalist, but to no avail.

JS: "Is that your job? You just talked about being a journalist!
CM: "Yeah, it is my job. My job is to help this country."

Compared to Matthews' some journalists attempted verbal restraint, though their true feelings were on full display in their body language and tone. Soledad O'Brien of CNN was so enamored with Michelle Obama in a 2007 interview that she never broke her clown like smile the whole eight minutes. Even Michelle Obama had a look on her face as if to ask, "Are you okay?"

Americans rarely learned anything new from so called interviews with Obama. One could almost recite his life's story from Kenya to Hawaii and Indonesia and back in a mere four week's time. The same excerpts from Obama's life story, his books, and his feverish calling to change the world were replayed and recycled as news. When ABC's Charles Gibson interviewed Obama on *World News Tonight*, the toughest question he asked candidate Obama was, "Barack, what kind of hubris is this that 'I am thinking about being President'?" Other questions were little more than a personal story segment where Gibson attempted to makes us feel that he was asking questions we desperately need and wanted to know the answer to. Says Gibson, "Your mom comes from the Pacific Northwest, migrates to Hawaii, goes to college there, right away, meets a dashing young Kenyan, gets pregnant and the result -... "That's me, says, Obama. The interview continues in this direction with how he and Michelle met and onto his daughters. Not one question up front on Obama's plans in his role as commander in chief in the face of two wars.

The Preacher and the Plumber

Two incidents in which the media most betrayed the American people were the handling of the Jeremiah Wright tapes and Obama's own socialist diatribe in his conversation with Joe Wurzelbacher, also known as Joe the Plumber. And, even though there are other stories the media spun, botched, and tried to ignore such as ACORN, Obama's slip about his "Muslim faith" and his connection to terrorist and extremist, Bill Ayers, which reveal their bias and disregard for the truth, these two incidents were the turning points in my own personal opinion of Obama's ability to be President of America.

The media bobbed and weaved to avoid the truth. Anchors and networks gave Jeremiah Wright a platform to become the victim. The leftist media tried to divert American's attention away from the main issue and towards race. Further, they tried to drag an ordinary American citizen through the mud for asking a question the media had not the nerve to ask. These two instances display the height of their deviousness, the depths of their idolatry to Obama, and the contempt they hold for their own country and the American voter.

Jeremiah Wright

"We bombed Hiroshima, we bombed Nagasaki, and we nuked far more than the thousands in New York and the Pentagon, and we never batted an eye... and now we are indignant, because the stuff we have done overseas is now brought back into our own front yards. America's chickens are coming home to roost."

"And the United States of America government, when it came to treating her citizens of Indian descent fairly, she

31

failed. She put them on reservations. When it came to treating her citizens of Japanese descent fairly, she failed. She put them in internment prison camps. When it came to treating her citizens of African descent fairly, America failed. She put them in chains, the government put them on slave quarters, put them on auction blocks, put them in cotton field, put them in inferior schools, put them in substandard housing, put them in scientific experiments, put them in the lowest paying jobs, put them outside the equal protection of the law, kept them out of their racist bastions of higher education and locked them into positions of hopelessness and helplessness. The government gives them the drugs, builds bigger prisons, passes a three-strike law and then wants us to sing 'God Bless America.' No, no, no, not God Bless America. God damn America — that's in the Bible — for killing innocent people. God damn America, for treating our citizens as less than human. God damn America, as long as she tries to act like she is God, and she is supreme. The United States government has failed the vast majority of her citizens of African descent"

"[The United States] government lied about their belief that all men were created equal. The truth is they believed that all white men were created equal. The truth is they did not even believe that white women were created equal, in creation nor civilization. The government had to pass an amendment to the Constitution to get white women the vote. Then the government had to pass an equal rights amendment to get equal protection under the law for women. The government still thinks a woman has no rights over her own body, and between Uncle Clarence who sexually harassed Anita Hill, and a closeted Klan court, that is a throwback to the 19th century, handpicked by Daddy Bush, Ronald Reagan, Gerald Ford, between Clarence and that stacked court, they are about to undo Roe vs. Wade, just like they are about to un-do affirmative action. The government lied in its founding documents and the government is still lying today. Governments lie."

In addition to what is listed here, Wright spewed hatred time and again with statements such as, "matters of national stupidity, "I mean security." He would refer to former Secretary of State Condoleezza Rice - a brilliant and accomplished woman notwithstanding her political career - as "Condoskeezer." And, finally he would refer to the United States and the US of KKK.

I won't lie. Re-watching the Jeremiah Wright tapes and reading the transcripts to write this part of the book nearly made me weep and it made me angry. I was embarrassed then just as I am embarrassed now reading it again. I am embarrassed as both black and American to know that each Sunday our people are being subjected to hate speech under the guise of gospel and God's holy name. Wright was seen rocking his hips back and forth while talking of "riding dirty," and speaking of damning of a country all under the guise of God.

That Barack Obama wanted to become President of a country that his mentor and minister for twenty years despised, was in my mind, unthinkable. The jig was up: not only was Barack Obama inexperienced and untested politically and professionally, but he also believed and accepted the worst about America – the very country he would swear to protect and honor. I was done and knew in my heart that most Americans would be done too - until the media dug deep to convince them otherwise.

The expose' on Jeremiah Wright was Obama's Monica Lewinsky. It was Obama's Titanic, his Swift Boat. The tapes that we heard all over the Internet and news media were indefensible. As much as the media and Obama tried to distance Obama from Wright, we all knew that this isn't the way a man of God behaves. We also knew that someone doesn't go unaffected listening to hate speech indoctrination for over twenty years. Jeremiah Wright's words were ugly to put it mildly, but they also revealed a hatred for our country. What's worse, one of the sermons was given September 16, 2001, just five short days following one of the most brutal attacks on our country. Instead of ministering to the power of love to heal, Wright unleashed another vicious attack on America, his tongue as a sword.

It would be several days before major news networks other than Fox News Channel seriously reported on the tapes. MSNBC, CNN, CNBC only spoke lightly of a church scandal, a church Barack Obama attended. Additionally, the media sought to dismiss the tapes as sound bites taken out of context. Writes editor-in-chief of Salon.com Joan Walsh, "the whole idea that Wright has been attacked over 'sound bites…" Walsh would have Americans believe Wright was being attacked. Wright became the victim in all of this and soon too was Barack Obama. The media quickly diminished Wright as a mere acquaintance. They sought to put Americans on the defensive questioning pointedly, "how many of you agree with everything your preacher says and does?" They distanced Obama's intimate ties to Wright whittling his twenty years of family like ties to little more than a case of guilt by association. Would it be fair to judge Obama and blame him for something he didn't say or do? And furthermore, Obama wasn't actually present during the sermons we saw. Childish and reckless defenses like these continued all the while ignoring the fact that Obama's book title, *The Audacity of Hope* was borrowed from Wright's sermons.

As backlash from the tapes grew, some networks took their denial to downright boldness of refusal to address. CNN's John Roberts host of "American Morning" laid it on the line by prefacing his interview with Obama this way, "I want to just stipulate at the beginning of this interview, we are declaring a Reverend Wright –free zone today. So, no questions about Reverend Wright. Our viewers want us to move on...so this morning, we're going to move on. Is that okay with you?" Obama smiled knowingly saying, "fair enough. That sounds just fine." Suddenly, questions about nuclear proliferation were important. Only, Obama STILL did not answer:

JR: If Iran attacked Israel with a nuclear weapon, would you use the United States' nuclear   arsenal against Iran?"

BO: "John, I'm not going to speculate.

June 2010 would prove that the left based media had been biased in reporting on Jeremiah Wright all along. A secret journalist email server called "Journolist" was discovered. Some three hundred journalists from major news organizations including *Politico*, *TIME*, *The New Republic*, *The Baltimore Sun*, *The Huffington Post*, and *The New Republic*, were strategizing on how to spin or make the Jeremiah Wright story disappear altogether. And, if they couldn't spin it, they would inflict Americans with race.

"Fred Barnes, Karl Rove, who cares - and call them racists. What is necessary is to raise the cost on the right of going after the left." Spencer Ackerman, formerly of the New Republic, now of Wired.

Joe the Plumber

By October 2008 the clock was running down and the election was just a month away with Obama's popularity slipping. Though the media cleaned up well behind Wright, Obama's campaign had taken a beating and many Obama faithful, including the media, wanted to get the vote done before the numbers got worse.

On October 13, 2008 Joe Wurzelbacher set out to accomplish what the media would not: have a candid

35

discourse with Obama on a tough question. According to his interview with Katie Couric, Joe would try to "corner" Obama in his neighborhood and ask the "tough" questions the media wasn't asking. And having had all his media interviews softly scripted, Obama slipped up catastrophically in this unprompted conversation. Obama revealed his true philosophy of capitalism and social justice. It was a telling insight into his socialist desires for America and the distance between his values and those of America.

It was a classic case in Obama's defense of the 'little guy' syndrome. After going 'round and 'round and trying to convince Joe that his plan would DECREASE taxes for the RIGHT people, Obama finally let known his Marxist heart, "not that I want to punish your success, I just want to give those folks behind you a chance. I think when you spread the wealth around, it's good for everybody." BOOM, BOOM, POW!

Well done, Joe. Joe got more than his five minutes from the exchange. And to Americans who were beginning to see the light, Joe's pushback that Obama was punishing the American dream made a lot of sense. This time – unequivocally and emphatically - in Obama's own words America had proof that Obama did not share American values and ideas in common. Still, Joe was no match for the media who focused single mindedly on discrediting the conversation, Joe's credibility, and his life. If Joe really was a plumber, he would need a mighty wrench because the media was about to throw him the kitchen sink. They had history to make and a naive plumber with cow jumping over the moon dreams of making a quarter million dollars a year wasn't about to stand in their way.

The media took their cues from Obama who soon after poked fun at McCain for fighting for the plumber and the plumber himself for his naiveté. A laughing crowd urged Obama on as he mocked in query, "How many plumbers do you know who make a quarter million dollars a year?" (So much for the audacity of hope.) After the plumber interview Obama was smug. With the media setting ablaze Joe the plumber's life, Obama self-righteousness was on fire. Instead of addressing the words and sentiments of Barack Obama's economic philosophy or the fact that what he said was socialist in nature, media journalists would attack and break down Joe the plumber as, well, a plumber.

Katie Couric wanted to know how the $250k tax would affect Joe the plumber. CNN anchor Rick Sanchez treated Joe like a child. His tone was dismissive and he in fact stated that viewers had been asking, why CNN had even been talking about Joe the plumber, yet here he was interviewing him. With gleeful reproach his first question was, why would you be upset by people making $250k a year when you aren't making that any time soon, are you?"

Diane Sawyer took it a step further putting the integrity of Joe's discourse with Obama in question. "And the McCain camp, some people have said they did contact you and tell you that you were going to be a major part of this, and had they contacted you before that encounter with Senator Obama?"

Joe answered, "Oh no, no, no one's contacted me as far as if I was going to be on the debate or as far as my name being used. No. I have been contacted by them and asked to show up at a rally. But other than that, no. I just happened to be here and Barack Obama happened to show up."

The handling of Joe the plumber revealed the depths of the media's and Barack Obama's contempt for the actual little guy who they swore Obama was trying to save. They could be no more indebted to the little guy than the man on the moon. The fact is Joe the plumber could have been any one of us. The leftist media would attack the citizens of this country who dare ask a question they didn't approve rather than have real truth come out. That Obama would laugh at a voter's dreams and ridicule the little guy to make a point was a cold blooded and calculating. His ruse of hope and change was thrown smack in the face of the American people.

THE RIVALS

What the media did to clean up Obama's mess after Jeremiah Wright, setting him up with softball journalism, and discrediting Joe the plumber would seem like patty cake compared to the way they treated Obama's rivals. Any formidable competition was hit with their very own WMD, Weapon of Media Destruction. Bill and Hillary Clinton, long time media favorites would be discarded as "entitled been there and done that." John McCain, previously adored by the media as a maverick would be subjected to ageism and dismissed as the white status quo. But no one, I mean no one would get the media's nostrils flaring like Sarah Palin.

The Clintons

Even though the media once wanted Americans to believe Hillary Clinton was the smartest woman in the world and came to her defense during Bill Clinton's sex "scandals," once Obama announced he would seek the Democratic nomination, the tables turned. Wisecracks about her pantsuits took center. Whereas staying with her marriage with Bill showed strength, now was weak and/or calculating. Where the scandals were of little consequence to the media at the time, they now threatened to tarnish Hillary's tough as nails image.

The media used divide and conquer tactics hoping to create new wounds asking, "What if Bill Secretly Wants Hillary to Lose?" During debates Hillary would get the tough questions first, and finally her exasperation led to impatiently calling the media out on its soft and cuddly treatment of Obama. "I do find it curious, and if anybody saw *Saturday Night Live*, you know, maybe we should ask Barack if he's comfortable and needs another pillow." Some laughed; others booed. The media sat back and waited for comedy and entertainment shows to finish it off. And, although Hillary was telling the truth - and everyone knew it- she'd failed the "take it like a man" test. A forced error victory for Obama and the media.

Because Hillary had the name, the backers, the historical making (at first) the money (at first) she would be the obvious choice in the three-way between her, John Edwards and unknown, inexperienced junior senator Barack Obama. She clearly underestimated the situation. Obama's love affair with the media was not a casual fling; this was true, obsessive love. Obama was not the rookie junior senator who got lucky in getting his Senate seat after Jack Ryan's scandal broke out. Oh, no. Hillary discovered quickly that with the media's help Obama was quickly able to upstage her and defuse her assets.

- The name: The Clinton name became trite and synonymous with dynasties of old: Bush, Clinton, Bush, Clinton. This only made Obama's change seem all the more necessary. Even Hillary's clever remark that after another Bush in the White House, "it would take another Clinton to clean it up" came across as desperate by the time the media was done.

- The backers: Her backers jumped ship to join the Obama hope and change train. Long time allies and "friends" such as Ted and Caroline Kennedy would pick Obama's side. And, the media would too. When Bill Clinton said that a vote for Obama was to "roll the dice" the media went in for the kill. After all these years of soulfully being the first black President, he was now just an old-establishment racist.

- The history: the only bigger history than a female President is the first African-American one. *Duh?!*

- And, money: with the backers, so went the money. And, Obama like no one before was able to raise an unprecedented amount of money. Never mind one of the first ways he was supposed to usher in change was to abide by voluntary contribution limits to make the game fair. He did not. The media never called him out on this, but backed him up in justifying that his moment was just too important to play fair, or, stand by his word. After all *he* was the little guy fighting for the other little guys against the big, bad, Clinton machine.

On every level, the media went bananas for Barack and their relationship with the Clintons was a blip on the radar screens of the past. Their attitude was that she'd had her moment in the sun and for that she should be grateful. They were moving on and Hillary and Bill may as well get used to it and for that matter, get with the program.

John McCain

Once Obama secured the Democratic nomination and McCain the Republican, the media work got a bit easier. McCain posed no real threat to Obama and the media knew it. Even with his decorated Vietnam service and his previously revered maverick status, they would remind voters of his age at every opportunity, 72 at the time. McCain would further help them along by trying to play up on his similarity to Obama: he would also raise taxes; McCain agreed with cap and trade. (McCain was failing miserably with his conservative base in order to keep the peace with the media who tolerated him as long as he was no threat to Obama.) And, so, without any history to be made in yet another white man taking the oath, McCain was treated as little more than a formality on the road to history in making Barack Obama the 44th President of the United States.

When Barack Obama chose Joe Biden as his running mate, it came off as a strange pick considering the abundance in juvenile blunders Biden made in referring to Obama as "clean" and "articulate." More than this, the skipping over Hillary Clinton revealed the frailty of Obama's ego. The media made do with Biden building him up as the regular guy who takes the train into Capitol Hill (from his mansion in Connecticut) just like the little guy. Ain't that tough enough?

As the media speculated who John McCain would choose a rundown of the usual suspects dominated the discussion: John Thune of South Dakota, Florida Governor Charlie Christ, Louisiana Governor Bobby Jindal, or ex-senator Fred Thompson. Nothing to see here. Mc Cain sauntered along somewhat easily, receiving polite albeit curt treatment of the mainstream press. That is until he made a choice that would live up to his maverick moniker.

On August 29, 2008 John McCain announced that Governor of Alaska Sarah Palin would join him on the Republican ticket. "She's got the grit, integrity, good sense and fierce devotion to the common good that is exactly what we need in Washington today," McCain said to a crowd of 15,000 in Ohio. McCain/Palin had finally breathed life into this election and put some competition in the game. His conservative base was well pleased and donations flooded in. McCain had given himself a much better shot at the presidency.

Initially, the media was caught off guard and scrambled to catch up to the name they did not authorize John McCain to pick. After seeing the enthusiasm from the

Republican base and the positive reaction from the American people, it would not take them long to regain their footing and unleash the whole of their fury on Sarah Palin.

Sarah Palin

Palin gave an immediate boost to the McCain campaign. Before announcing Palin as his running mate, the media could finally coast a bit and start deliberating clever lines worthy of election night to mark the history of the first black president. Sure, the media was busy putting out fires here and there: the Jeremiah Wright scandal left a mark and Americans were starting to come forward demanding to know, "where's the beef." Before Palin there had been no issue wide enough, no person high enough since the early days of Clinton when he was struggling to secure the nomination, to keep Obama out of the White House.

Sarah Palin changed that and the game too. Most Americans and particularly conservatives liked her off the bat. Her plain spoken and down to earth manner made her an instant hit with those mid-West and Southern states that Obama was struggling to win over before the election. States like Kansas, Missouri, Kentucky, Virginia, and Arkansas were in serious play. And as Governor of a big oil state, she as a Vice Presidential candidate had something that even the Democratic Presidential candidate didn't have: experience and credibility on energy issues. The chatter about town was that Sarah Palin was the real deal whereas Obama was only pretending. Palin *was* fresh. She *was* of the people. Palin was a proven leader. She was a trailblazer and a Governor.

Seeing the changing tide, the media went to work. The McCain campaign decided that Katie Couric, newly crowned anchoress of the "CBS Evening News" would get the first Palin interview. The stakes were high for both sides. Couric's edited and mocking interview set the tone for the rest of the campaign where the media would instantly portray Palin as a lightweight, twist her words, call out her children, attack her as a mother, make fun of her vernacular, and even dismiss her political clout as if Alaska were not even a real state.

Couric's question of what newspapers Palin read was an obvious set-up for a big Palin fumble. For even if Palin had answered the question expertly, the question itself implied illiteracy on several fronts.

In live coverage following the Vice Presidential debate, Couric remarked, "Everyone was waiting to see how the political newcomer would do tonight and perhaps the headline is Governor Sarah Palin did not embarrass herself or her running mate as some Republicans might have feared and some Democrats might have hoped." Palin was not an embarrassment and the media knew it. She was clicking most with who mattered: the American people, voters. The media was very afraid. They had to pass that fear onto McCain and the voters even if it meant that they would in turn be calling millions of American voters inept as well. The media made it their mission to plant great seeds of doubt in the minds of the McCain campaign and other Republicans on whether or not she was good enough. To a large degree they succeeded.

In interviewing John McCain on the "CBS Evening News," Couric says, " I spoke with your running mate, Sarah Palin, and she told me that if action is not taken, A Great Depression is quote 'the road that America may find itself on'…is that the kind of language Americans need to be hearing right now? (Did anyone ask Obama if it was a good idea for Joe Biden to ask a man in a wheelchair to stand up?)

I don't presume to know the inner workings of the McCain camp, but it appeared John McCain took the bait. Had I been an advisor on his team, I would have pointed out to him this. Before Sarah Palin the media was soft on him because he was not perceived as a threat to Barack. If Palin were ineffective in resonating with voters, the media would laugh behind their backs and treat her kindly in public. Kind of the same way they treat Snookie from Jersey Shore, or Paula Abdul. That the media grabbed hold of Sarah's ankles and would not let go was all the proof the McCain camp needed: They were cooking with HOT grease now!!

Instead McCain freaked out that Palin was a liability. Just as Obama had succeeded in his divide and conquer strategy against America's social classes, the media succeeded in dividing the Republican Party by the lines of their elite and ordinary conservative folks. These ordinary folks, the Republican base, longed to see someone with good old fashioned conservative values, not just a fancy degree from a fancy place with a fancy last name. McCain never got it that while Palin was not perfect, she had a pulse on the nation's thirst for conservatism. The media sensed this and continued to press the judgment of McCain in selecting Palin. As McCain became defensive and nervous struggling to maintain his favor with the press, it appeared he conceded the media's assessment of Palin. Palin began looking tentative and unsteady with herself not knowing who she was supposed to be.

The secret was that the media did not dislike or disrespect Palin for any lack of pedigree or political experience. It wasn't even her popularity with American voters that truly unnerved the media. Her values are what ate them alive and kept them up at night plotting her demise. To begin with, Palin is strongly pro-life as evidenced by her decision (not just in political rhetoric) to give birth to a Down syndrome baby in her forties. This scared the left tremendously as they worried what might happen should she be an inspiration to other women who got the holier than thou idea that they should accept a cross like a baby with down syndrome as a gift from God, rather than do what the media had told them was perfectly normal and fine all along: abort it. She was threatening to destroy all the progress they'd made over the last thirty years. Suppose women started to feel guilty about killing their own child. The left wing media could not tolerate her filling the heads of women with this holy-roller nonsense. Feminism should be about the power of a woman to choose so long as she doesn't make the wrong choice, which is to give life to the life she created if it be a burden to her own life. Yes, Palin was a problem indeed.

The media would eventually work Palin over so vehemently, that in the end it would require too much conviction and courage for McCain/Palin to put up the necessary fight they would need in each subsequent battle to win the war. John McCain was worn down and couldn't go the distance. Like the American people, he gave up and gave in too soon. Hope and change would prevail over conservative values yet again. In reward for McCain conceding to Obama early, the media put the weight of the McCain/Palin loss on Sarah Palin while McCain retreated in quiet reflection of what could have been. Palin took the hit on all sides. McCain stood by and watched.

ADDENDUM

This section needed "The Lovers," section as well as "The Haters," to include Fox News Channel and most right wing internet publications who couldn't find one good, or sensible thing to say about Obama— the man or the policy—and thus fanned the flames of discord to unbearable levels.

I've since learned how both sides of the media have their faults and untenable bias. To a fault, they support and air opinions that bolster their status quo beliefs and candidates and to rile and divide rather than inform and improve the world. You may be quicker than me. Knowing this all along and thinking I couldn't possibly have been so naive not to have seen this much earlier and to have known this while I was in it. I hear you and have spun many cycles about my right-wing blindness. But, I can assure you this ignorance is commonplace in ideologues and is therefore worth mentioning.

We don't know what we don't know. And sadly, many of us will never dig deeply enough into our beliefs and motivations to find out a sliver of what we don't. One of my favorite speakers Lisa Nichols says you cannot un-know what you learn. Being in the arena revealed truths about the media I simply didn't know or couldn't face as a pundit. I know much more now, but I'm aware mostly of all that I cannot know. I've since shut down the news media in my life save for the occasional brief headline or major happening in the world. It's the beginning to a peace that surpasses all human understanding. I promise you.

Some have described the media as a circus. But circus performers are artists. All know it to be highly styled entertainment...for kids. The media is more like WWF wrestling. A highly choreographed performance programmed for adults to drive fear and scarcity mindedness. Stylized to appeal to our desperate need to believe we are in control and know best. Knowing my own error and the lie most of it is, I now see every jab, kick, attack, and incredulous facial gesture and slight of the head for what it is. Show.

CHAPTER THREE

Obama

"There can be no deep disappointment where there is no love"

Martin Luther King, Jr.

You are reading a book by a conservative who loves Barack Obama and therefore, I am as disappointed today as I was November 4, 2008. As I stood in my election booth choosing to vote McCain/Palin, it was a painful moment knowing that I would not vote on this side of history. I knew that Obama would win and I knew how much America wanted this moment. And even though I am a conservative, I wanted the moment too. I would not vote for the first African-American President. What's worse is that I loved him since meeting him that stunning night in 2004. But a lot happened since 2004 and so in that booth, I was done kidding myself with Barack Obama.

No matter how wise we are today and how we pride ourselves on our good choices, we have all played the fool in a relationship at least once in our lives. It's that relationship where you were so blinded by the lights that you had no idea that you were generating all that electricity on your own. Sure, they may have encouraged you at first, but where they gave you an inch you could run marathon on that teeny whisper of what to come.

Our love affair with Barack Obama is no different. The only difference is our love affair with Obama was a full frontal display of Obama girl watching, thrill up the leg babbling, campaign festival. Obama took tens of millions of delusional lovers with him and left us all in a doleful haze of what could have been. We had such high hopes for this one. How could we have not seen it?

Of course, not having met you, I cannot be sure exactly what drinking your Kool-aid tasted or felt like. Mine was not syrupy sweet like lover Peggy Joseph caught on film exclaiming like a giddy child on Christmas morning, "I won't have to worry about putting gas in my car. I won't have to worry about paying my mortgage." Sweet still, my kool-aid washed down with expectations of unity, edification, and the courage beyond politics to crack down on the plight of the black family. Drinking my kool-aid brought comfort that his symbol as a black man in charge, would somehow change the face of time. Not as delusional as Peggy, but delusional enough to think he could be all I hoped for in a person and a politician.

BOSTON 2004
More than a feeling

The one night stand in Boston intoxicated America on Obama. The first thing I noticed when Barack Obama took the stage July 27, 2004 was that he was – I beg your pardon for the cliché – tall, perfectly dark, and staggeringly handsome. Even before he opened his mouth, I could hardly wait on the brilliance I knew was coming. Obama didn't disappoint. In his first sentence he talked of Lincoln, gratitude, privilege, and honor. He spoke of his Kenyan father – so that's where he gets those cheekbones – and his Kansan mother, both passed on. When he spoke of our American genius, and he spoke of his love for us, I was out of my chair. "I stand here knowing…that in no other country on earth, is my story even possible. Tonight we gather to affirm the greatness of our nation, not because of the height of our skyscrapers, or the power of our military, or the size of our economy." As if he didn't already have us, he continued on to say that, "there's not a liberal

America and a conservative America – there's a United States of America. There's not a black America and a white America and a Latino America and Asian America; there's the United States of America!!!" The room was lit to their feet, as so many rooms were around the country that night.

By now, I was nearly in tears. My grandmother Vernell died in 2000. I mourned my loss all over again knowing how seeing this Senator from Chicago would send her over the moon with pride and joy. And, Michelle too. I thought back to 1984 when Jesse Jackson began a run for President how she and my grandfather relished with pride, albeit subdued, at this bold statement. While Jackson's run was a great symbol of the dream coming true, most Americans undoubtedly knew that the time had not yet come and that he was not the one. On this night, just twenty years later, Barack Obama represented a secure place for her hopes and dreams of a black man becoming President of the United States. Though we were watching a keynote address to the Democratic convention for John Kerry and John Edwards in 2004, even your cat could have told you that night we were looking at the new great American hope in 2008.

So as Obama spoke I continued talking with my grandmother Vernell from high above, feeling her with us. I would high five her on the best punch lines, or, go "*uummm, uuumm, ummmm*, when Obama really scratched an itch. (Umm, umm, umm is the East Texas equivalent to OMG!) Keeping my hands in the air with each poised turn of the head and definitive tilt of the jaw, just watching him that night; so many dreams had already come true. The icing on the cake? Michelle. Obama's wife looked like me. She was also African-American and unambiguously so. He had married one of us. It was almost too much to ask. It was a black Camelot. That night left us all stalking him for more.

Obama was a willing and beautiful target. We chased and he encouraged us – never evasive or aloof, still never fully ours yet. Our indulgence seemed his pleasure. We found out that his speech was just the beginning. His star was rising amid unsuspecting eyes. He was the first black President of the Harvard Law Review. And, even if we didn't know what that meant, we knew if he accomplished it, it must have been important. We discovered and quickly purchased a book he wrote in 1995, *Dreams from my Father*. Then in 2006, he answered our calls for more of him with *The Audacity of Hope*. Our hearts growing fonder and love deepened.

But blinded by our infatuation our love from that night lingered on and we kept hearing and seeing everything through the lens of that night in Boston. We wanted more of THAT Barack Obama. And so on February 10, 2007, Barack Obama would finally give us what we had all been waiting for; he announced that he would run for President.

Obama's Words

One of my favorite Chris Rock skits is, "He speaks So Well," which is a funny take on white people's reaction to a well spoken black man. The black man at that time was Colin Powell. Still, when someone says "he speaks so well" when talking about Obama, it is so very true that it isn't patronizing. It's like saying the Williams' sisters are athletic – well, because they are. They are also smart, crafty tennis players, but their power and athleticism stands alone. So it is with Obama's speaking prowess. He is smart. He is witty. He may also be athletic, but to hear him speak is to first think how well he does so and how articulate he is compared to most of us. He had such a way with words, Obama, that when he spoke, specifically in 2004 and throughout the campaign, one could become mesmerized in rhetoric and posture. It wasn't just speaking; he was a brilliant storyteller with poignant and inspiring connections to the listener.

An uncharacteristic trait for a politician, Obama avoided corners of anger, negativity, or resentment. Where his name was funny, he spoke of it meaning "blessing." Where there was shortsightedness or worry, he spoke of the work we have left to be done, "we have more work to do."

He was criticized often during the campaign for being all about speeches and he would come back with, "words matter". Indeed they do, as long as we mean what we speak. His words gave us an awareness of our own vision and there was Obama's power. When he spoke, he inspired us to our own inner voice of hope. He called America a "magical place." "It is because men and women of every race, from every walk of life, continued to march for freedom long after Lincoln was laid to rest, that today we have the chance to face the challenge of this millennium together, as one people – as Americans." His words lent us beauty inside and out.

It wasn't just the words themselves, but there was the supreme being of his presence. My grandmother would talk often of poise – she was into pageants after all. Poise isn't a teachable habit to most people. Barack Obama has the poise to convey all the promise and intention of his words. Some say it can be in the chin, the jaw line, or the shoulders. It could be all of these. Whatever it is, his words are born out of his poise. His poise goes beyond speaking "so well" and gives his words and speeches a swagger superior to most others.

Obama's Story

"That is the true genius of America, a faith in the simple dreams of its people, the insistence on small miracles. That we can tuck in our children at night and know they are fed and clothed and safe from harm. That we can say what we think, write what we

51

think, without hearing a sudden knock on the door. That we can have an idea and start our own business without paying a bribe or hiring somebody's son. That we can participate in the political process without fear of retribution, and that our votes will he counted - or at least, most of the time." Barack Obama

Obama's story was the better half to his words. Obama's greatest appeal wasn't just what he said, but was that he was the one saying it. Black and white, but not in the tragic and oppressed way American mixed race is often portrayed. Obama wore his mixed heritage with pride and confidence. His story was exotic and lovely. It was a life that seemed full of worldly experience that blessed him with a third eye. So that when he talks about America's genius, he almost does so as an outsider with the ability to appreciate what we have long taken for granted. Saying we can start our own business without paying a bribe and dissent without fearing a knock on the door are things that most Americans never considered a privilege before hearing him acknowledge it as such in 2004. His background weighted in us a deeper sense of pride and understanding of our freedoms.

The enticing part of his story was less about race and more about the authority of worldly calm he exuded. The style was cool, but not cocky. He was handsome, but quick with self-deprecation of his big ears and funny name. He was humble, but confident enough to throw some of his extra our way. All of these elements are in his story from living abroad and island style to being the first black editor of the Harvard Law Review and on to being a community organizer in Chicago. Who knew Kansas and Kenya could get on so well. Apart from each other they are Dorothy and runners, blended together a dynamic and inspiring story.

Obama's Family Values

Obama was and is a family man. I cringe as I write this truth, but in choosing Michelle (or her choosing him) he did wonders for the image of the black family and the black woman. He also did a favor to himself on issues of race and relationships in both the black and white community.

Black women are often portrayed as the loud mouthed, sassy, hand on the hip shrew who is no use to a successful man of any color. The way it often goes (and we've come to expect it so) is that most successful, tall, dark, and handsomes end up with Blondie (or a black woman so fair skinned her race is ambiguous: OJ Simpson, Van Jones, Tiger Woods, Quincy Jones, Sidney Poitier, Clarence Thomas, Kobe Bryant.. Though there is not a thing wrong with it on this green earth, it subconsciously underscores the notion that black women don't fit in elite circles. No matter what anyone says, even today, that image of the successful black man with the white wife still leaves black women out on a limb as an inadequate complement to a successful man. All of us know that the woman on a successful man's arm is a show of pride. Every time a black woman sees yet another successful black woman with the white wife, we get the message. We feel the sting of not being good enough for up there. You don't have to take my word for it. Read *Essence* and *Ebony* magazine, or listen to the lyrics of Kanye West's, "Golddigger."

Not Barack Obama. He answered so many black women's (chocolate women's) prayers in being married to Michelle. Michelle is a beautiful, educated, tall, fit, fashionable woman. Furthermore, it is imperative to note that this black woman is a star in her own right. She is from a strong, character driven family, highly educated, and smart. So smart that she didn't simply fall for Obama's words or his story. She would have her brother approve him on the basketball court before agreeing to date. Michelle's is an image unseen nationally in America since

Claire Huxtable of "The Cosby Show." Americans loved Dr. Claire Huxtable, the beautiful and intelligent black matriarch of the eighties, but critics, both black and white continually pointed out that she was fictional and therefore, unrealistic. Michelle is our proof that Claire can be just as real in our lives as she was in our hearts. For that reality, the black community and white community loved Michelle and Barack both.

Together, their story as a family is just as beautiful. I am no body language expert but most can tell that the Obama's have an uncontrived bond and closeness rarely seen in politics. They aren't like the sappy sweet Al and Tipper story: the high school or college sweethearts. Not like the Clintons who give off the convenient kind of coupling who are married not only to one another but to a lifetime of political ambition and legacy. Neither are they the James Carville and Mary Matalin duo playing up on the gimmick of opposites attract in love as in politics. Though politics and marriage often go hand in hand, it's nice to see the real deal. The deal that gives voters the gut feeling that a good union is good sense and stability we can trust.

The Obama's family values are a display of the American dream. Michelle and Barack showed us a young couple building on success, with high hopes and expectations for themselves, their family, and their country.

Obama's Personality

You know those highly intelligent, witty people, who appear to have it all but still manage not to take themselves too seriously. They don't squabble neurotically over the gray eggs that arrived cold (me), or fiercely argue a point in a conversation even when most at the table know they are right, or at least want them to be (me, again). Such was the charm and the personality of the Barack Obama we met in 2004-2007.

People would often say that Bill Clinton also had this charm – the ability to make someone feel as if they were the only one in the room. The difference with Obama is that the person feels the energy of *everyone* in the room. Obama's presence sparked an excitement because he came off as one of the people. He was so laid back and easy. He was always careful to pay more attention to those in the crowd instead of himself, "I know you didn't come here just for me," when speaking to his supporters at his announcement to run. "I made lasting friendships here- friends I see in the audience today."

We forgave him for bowling a thirty-seven (balls down the gutter) while trying to woo blue collar voters in Pennsylvania. We forgive that because we love someone with enough confidence to try where they know they will most certainly fail.

Despite an elite education, an exotic background full of wise enlightenment, and phenomenal family, Obama came across as this ordinary down to earth guy who just happens to be running for President of the United States of America.

WHAT HAPPENED

Trying to rationalize a good love gone bad is a tenuous spot. The hard part is accepting that the love was never true. When the flags show up, we make excuses and say anyone can have a bad day, or week, right? When we are blown off, we curse ourselves for being too pushy. Your mom always said you were the needy one. The case is usually that the same things that hooked us are the exact same things that will put us off.

Everything Obama offered us in the way of his words, his story, his family, and his personality was changed completely as he was campaigning for our hand in political matrimony. And after he was sworn in, those characteristics we loved all but vanished.

Words Matter

Obama's showed us with his speech in Boston that he was an incredible orator and more than this he had a command for using words to illicit feelings and sentiment. Words mattered. As his words were so good, we began to hang on to each one. Unfortunately, that night in Boston would be the last time his words conveyed love and reverence for America and her people. In nearly all speeches after it, his tone and words took on a new context of mild finger pointing, flaw searching bitterness.

The change in words and tone began subtly in 2007 when he announced his candidacy and has increased ever since to the present where he boldly admonishes us. Take this very first indication starting with his announcement to run for president on February 10, 2007.

> "We all made this journey for a reason. It's humbling, but in my heart I know you didn't come here just for me, you came here because you believe in what this country can be. In the face of war, you believe there can be peace. In the face of despair, you believe there can be hope. In the face of a politics that's shut you out, that's told you to settle, that's divided us for too long, you believe we can be one people, reaching for what's possible, building that more perfect union."
>
> Barack Obama

Suddenly we're "shut out, settling, and divided." 'A more perfect union?" Didn't the founding fathers already establish this? Obama would borrow this line over and over to convey to us that we were incomplete. See, in 2004 we were already perfect. We were perfect enough for his story to only be possible here. Now in this first pronouncement to unite with us, we are beginning to be made aware of our flaws, "… perfecting our unions, usher in a new birth of freedom." Whereas before we were settling, with him our standards would be set to par. A *Washington Post* article appearing days after his announcement with a quote from Obama that says it all. "I want to win, but I just don't want to win. I want to transform this country."

Here Obama laid the first brick for his Hope and Change platform. It wasn't yet his slogan, but already he was focusing more on the change, or the transformation he had in mind. "The genius of our founders is that they designed a system of government that can be changed." "For it is our unyielding faith that in the face of impossible odds, people who love their country can change it." This is the one night stand that led to the marriage proposal where the guy says, "I want to marry you. And, make a more perfect you. In this announcement for President, there is not a single remnant of that unconditional love in Boston.

Whereas in Boston he focused on the solution without bitterness or negativity, here he spoke of "disillusionment" and "frustration." Still, Obama speaks of us fighting on together and that is good. Though this talk of unity would also soon change. It wasn't long before Obama's campaign came branded the Hope and Change mantra."Yes We Can" (change). And, "Change We Can Believe In." You better believe it took an even shorter time for the message of Hope and Change to become a lecture.

He and Michelle both regularly began to use words divisively in the campaign. In March 2008, Michelle spoke in South Carolina feeling so confident about her ability to connect with black voters that she didn't use notes. She spoke seemingly from the heart. Nonetheless, after a brief small talk of her people originally being from South Carolina, she went quickly to the ugly. "We're a divided country, we're a country that is "just downright mean," we are "guided by fear," we're a nation of cynics, sloths, and complacents. "We have become a nation of struggling folks who are barely making it every day," she said, as heads bobbed in the pews. "Folks are just jammed up, and it's gotten worse over my lifetime." And, doggone it, I'm young. Forty-four!"

One of the worst instances in Obama's case was at a fundraiser in San Francisco. In responding to struggling states frustration with Government, Obama accused folks in Pennsylvania of bitterness saying and mocking them that not surprisingly, "they cling to guns and religion."

"We worship an awesome God in the Blue states…we have gay friends in the Red states."
Barack Obama, 2004

The Story

Americans took as much pride in Barack Obama's story as he did. So far we'd only been given the heart strings version (typical of one night stands). Soon more of his story unfolded revealing questionable acquaintances and contrasting philosophies to the American way. We had heard all about his rise from boyhood and up through the ranks from Harvard to community organizing. What was left out was the more recent contexts that influenced him today.

The parts of his story that went unplayed day after day were the most critical to know. Ones that would help put our feelings and his of late in proper perspective. Parts such as his relationships with Tony Rezko, Bill Ayers, and Jeremiah Wright. Those are the stories he was most recently living.

When cornered about a relationship and bad business deal with real estate developer Tony Rezko, Obama became defensive and snappy. Obama cast off his association with known terrorist turned professor Bill Ayers as an acquaintance he met at a fundraiser. And, Reverend Jeremiah Wright? He was dumped ceremoniously in an eloquent speech on race.

Several pieces of his story understandably gave logic to recent hints at bitterness: a fatherless home, being bounced around by his mother to Indonesia with a new husband and new siblings, and then to Hawaii to live with grandparents, but the confidence he once showed in his story seemed to turn into a desperate act to belong and to punish America for all the injustice he'd lived and seen in the world.

More and more it seemed he didn't know exactly who he was. He claimed Christianity as his religion, but then let a comment slip about his Muslim faith. At some point during the campaign, I believe when some blacks didn't think he was black enough, we noticed that his voice took on a Jesse Jackson like edge one guesses to appease a certain demographic of voters. It wasn't just his tone, it was his actual pronunciation. He began saying his-toh-ray, instead of history. Subtle, but enough to cause a brow to twitch and reveal his thinning veneer of confidence. Everywhere he went he was a different character playing Americans against each other coast to coast and using his story to help him.

Family Matters

I hoped Obama's family values would carry over into the American mainstream. I prayed he would be symbolic to the potential of black families in America. Selfishly, I saw him putting a team together to tackle the issue of the 70% out of wedlock birth rate, or at least going to a few schools to talk to young black men about the importance of staying in school, the responsibilities of sex and marriage. Seeing that he was patriarch of such a beautiful family, my hope was that pushing this possibility to the black community by example would be an imperative as president. I don't think this was so naïve.

He mentioned himself in 2004 that we must address a "black boy with a book as acting white." He also lamented,

"If there is a child on the southside of Chicago who can't read, that matters to me, even if it's not my child." So tender, so true. (Again, love, I say, love)

Well, I don't know if Derrion Albert was a good reader, but he was killed leaving Fenger High School on Chicago's South Side on September 24, 2009. Albert was beaten to death by students while several classmates stood ringside and watched failing to help or even be mortified. Most were cheering and jumping about ecstatic with their front row seats to the savage beating of their classmate.

Michelle Obama is from the South Side of Chicago. President Obama says he cares deeply for the South Side of Chicago where he began his legacy as a community activist. I'll never understand the judgment in their choosing to fly off to Denmark in an effort to bring the Olympics TO CHICAGO just days after a child was tragically murdered by his classmates. Olympic Games? How could a President who claimed to be so dialed in to injustice and the need for hope set any priority above being there for his Chicago brethren? Obama did not spend one day in the community grieving the loss of this honor student. Obama did not make a public announcement of any kind about the senseless violence plaguing the city. Instead he was off to Denmark to compete for an Olympics bid that few Americans wanted.

On September 28, 2009, Press Secretary Robert Gibbs came out saying that President Obama would address the Derrion Albert murder. Obama himself never once publicly addressed Albert's death. Instead Robert Gibbs announced on October 1, 2009 that Obama would dispatch cabinet members Secretary of Education Arne Duncan and Attorney General Eric Holder to Chicago. Did Duncan and Holder meet at a school gym with the people? Did they convene with the residents of Chicago's south side and communicate with Albert's mother, his teachers, or his friends in their neighborhood? Did they really give any indication to the community that they came to collaborate and help the people solve the problem of aimless and lost black youth on the southside of Chicago? Duncan and Holder held a meeting at the Four Seasons with community leaders and a few residents but not before leaving Fenger High school with a grant of $500,000. They cut a check and ran out on these kids, their families, and their own family values.

This sort of political apathy is the sort that would have started riots in the 1960s. This type of violence in a community back then would have sparked parents and preachers into action. That Obama all but ignored the incident personally and Albert's mom was rarely in the news and that there was little community outraged expressed is a telling display of just how little regard there is for the lives of young, poor, black children. This community and their children are resigned to accept a failing education system, tough streets, even death. Hope for these children to have a family and attention to their well-being seemed urgent here, not Olympic Games.

The bid for the Olympics had very little to do with hope and change that Americans had been waiting on from this President. Very little support for the Olympics was expressed during his campaign and as far as most could tell, with the economy the way it is, all this hoopla about health care reform, the stimulus, etc. Americans were not having Olympic dreams. Where Obama ended up failing miserably in Denmark chasing the love of the international community as their new global president, he missed the opportunity to show and receive love tenfold in where the enormity of his ability to make a difference to just one child may have made a world of difference to a life, to Chicago. That would have been change we could believe in!

Obama's Personality

In 2004 Obama skin appeared so thick, we imagined him taking the high road all of the time. The self proclaimed "skinny kid with big ears" smoothly self deprecated towards winning our confidence. We all get prickly sometimes, but there were times when he took an arrogant line most contrary and well beneath the man we fell in love with.

One such time was on the campaign where he told Hillary in front of the world, "You're likeable enough Hillary." It was a huge dig on Hillary who in fact does not come across as likeable. Though, it was a small slight, it was a gross display of poor character since until then had likeability to spare.

Obama has continually left the high road behind for the tones he promised to avoid: pettiness, cocky arrogance, and divisiveness. The best way to describe it all is petulance.

Just two days after Obama was sworn into office he took a meeting with Republican Congressional leaders. His response to their opposition to his stimulus plan: "I won. I'm the president." "You can't just listen to Rush Limbaugh and get things done." Nah, nana, *boo-boo*!!!

THE DEEP DISAPPOINTMENT

Two and a half years have flown by. The love all around is fading. Obama has very few backers in the American people, his political party, the media, and in his beloved global community. How could sentiment have changed so quickly and so dramatically since that night in 2004 and why is Obama unable to do anything to rectify the situation? It seems, even his speeches are disjointed and diffuse. His press conferences full of restatements and non apologetic apologies. His poise is little more than a superficial chin lift. And, his words and tone of voice is vexed and put upon. It seems right to say that our President got way more than he bargained for while we got way less.

Division and Derision

I think most of us, Obama included, have been surprised at how little Obama has succeeded in mending racial differences and curing prejudices the way his speeches implied. Obama is equally ineffective when it comes to unifying Americans in Americanism. In fact, our country is more divided than ever politically and racially.

During the election Obama got a lot of flak for saying that a question about abortion was "above of his pay grade." Even for a President, there are times when this is still true. Truthfully, his role does not require him to comment on every little or every big social and political issue of the day such as the Gates arrest, the mosque at Ground Zero, and heaven forbid Snookie as ladies of *The View* would ask him. But we were so enamored with him as a person that we eventually got TMI (too much information) from what was on his iPod to what he thought of Kayne West at the Video Music Awards: "jackass."

It just isn't necessary for the president to lecture incessantly as he does now and put his two cents in on every topic in what would Jesus do fashion. And, it hasn't worked for him or the country.

Race

His speech on race after the Jeremiah Wright incident was really a vague dismissal of Jeremiah Wright as being caught out of true character. Obama was also quick to drag his grandmother and the nation at large down with Reverend Wright and condemn us all as harborers of some racial resentment. Who doesn't spit racial epithets or vent prejudices outside of polite company? Obama observed. His grandmother who raised him after all was, "a woman who once confessed her fear of black men who passed her by on the street, and who on more than one occasion has uttered racial or ethnic stereotypes that made me cringe."

63

So because Reverend Wright got busted as a racist, all Americans now are angry, if not racists, only we've been good in polite company and haven't been caught by surprise?

Acting Stupidly

And, without his teleprompter - what we later learned was the key to his much of his smooth talk - Obama's speaking ability was retarded to your average reactionary babbling something akin to *Mystery Science Theatre*. This leads us to the "beer summit." Not only did our President prejudge the police officers who arrested a defiant Henry Louis Gates without having "all the facts," he said that the police "acted stupidly." Not satisfied with this conclusion - having "not been there" - Obama went on inflaming an already volatile racial situation by expanding his argument to America at large. "I think we know separate and apart from this incident is that there's a long history in this country of African-Americans and Latinos being stopped by law enforcement disproportionately. That's just a fact." So much for unity and moreover the part in his speech on race relations about "not succumbing to cynicism," or talking race "only as a spectacle."

His response in this matter was very disappointing as he was holding a press conference on health care. When the police officers and their chief pushed back on Obama's assertions, he would give himself a teachable moment and invite all involved to have a beer with him at the White House. The White House went about distracting us and making light of the egg dripping down Obama's face by creating a buzz over everyone's beer selection. While it was Miller time for them, unfortunately for us the damage to our country was done and Obama's opportunity to lend some cohesiveness – by staying out of it – towards racial issues lost.

Ground Zero

It isn't only racially, where Obama has failed to unify Americans. He has failed in simple Americanism. In addressing the controversy over the right of the Islamist church to build a mosque at Ground Zero, the site of the 9/11 terrorist attack, the President made sure to put Americans down. This time we needed to check our Constitution and emotional sensitivity to 9/11.

"The 9/11 attacks were a deeply traumatic event for our country and the pain and the experience of suffering by those who lost loved ones is just unimaginable. So I understand the emotions that this issue engenders. And ground zero is, indeed, hallowed ground." "But let me be clear. As a citizen, and as president, I believe that Muslims have the same right to practice their religion as everyone else in this country. And that includes the right to build a place of worship and a community center on private property in Lower Manhattan, in accordance with local laws and ordinances. This is America. And our commitment to religious freedom must be unshakable."

Nothing in our Obama's words fostered solidarity or unity. Nowhere in his posture was sensitivity to the hearts of New Yorkers. And, speaking of New Yorkers, wouldn't the proper response have been for him to leave this debate up to the people and leaders of New York? This is the problem with pedestals; so hard to come down.

Big Oil

When our President did have the responsibility to respond, take action and show leadership he showed petulance, indecision, and apathy to the extreme. It was clear that Obama was not into all that "buck stopping in the Oval office" jazz that he inherited from President Bush.

65

The BP Oil spill was President Obama's Hurricane Katrina. Polling indicated that nearly 52% of Americans dislike his handling of the oil spill, the same as Mr. Bush's handling of Hurricane Katrina. He petulantly pointed the finger in all directions except to himself. It took him almost a month to get down to the coast to check the spill out, and another to come up with an action plan to clean up and stop the spill. In the meantime, his process was to blame dependence on oil (us), and greedy BP executives with their yachts and big planes and big profits.

He auditioned the badass: "I am holding meetings so I'll know whose ass to kick."

He tried on sarcasm: "I can't go down to the ocean and suck up the oil with a straw?" Finally, he just did what he thought would satisfy everyone and declared he would, "make BP pay."

BP agreed to pay $20 billion dollars toward the cleanup of the spill and reimbursement to the Gulf. After meeting with Obama, the BP chairman held a press conference making sure to let Americans know that BP "cares for the small people." (Wonder where he got the notion that America was full of little guys?)

None of these responses cut the mustard in leadership, solidarity, or resolution. Obama certainly missed a chance to inspire confidence in his words, poise, or leadership. In the end, just saying everyone was working as diligently as they could to find a solution and get the fishing industry back to work, would have probably done it.

Instead it was politics as usual. Point the finger someplace else and use the incident as an excuse to barrel through an anti-drilling, anti-oil agenda. Namely, more laws, regulations, restrictions, and higher costs for the American taxpayer. There was nothing new about this tone in Washington. We knew it like the back of our hands.

Global Frenemies

What was new was the inside job Obama was doing on America abroad. Though we'd been properly warned that Obama saw himself as a global citizen and global President, I don't think we were ready for the approach Obama would take to endear himself internationally. Americans would have to be blamed and dismissed as arrogant bullies who like the rest of civilization bore the evil stain of slavery and ill treatment of the human race. He himself, not being responsible for that history, was not part of that America, however. With him at the helm as a global citizen, Obama assured the world that America would change and therefore the world, too.

To a crowd of about two-thousand in France, "In America there is a failure to appreciate Europe's leading role in the world...there have been times where America has shown arrogance, been dismissive, even derisive." Americans weren't even allowed to ask a question of their own President in the presence of French and German company. Our President further shunned us for the French and German students saying, "Do me a favor Americans, wait til' we get back home and I'll do a town hall there." Ouch.

And so it went from the beginning where Obama apologized for Americans to the world regarding slavery, to the Guantanamo Bay prison, to the war on terror, and even for our CIA. His initial appearances were so filled with making sure the world knew just how sorry America was that the media dubbed it as his apology tour.

Only this tour backfired miserably at home and abroad. Americans felt attacked and humiliated from within. The world saw a pompous, ego-maniac naïve enough to think he could obtain their love and loyalty with empty apologies and promises of American emasculation. Further, they instantly distrusted a leader who leads against his country's own interests. Though this trampling on America earned President Obama a Nobel Peace Prize, it was a dead end to constructive foreign and domestic relations.

Hypocrisy

In 2008 President Bush sent Americans a $600 tax stimulus to which Michelle mocked to a crowd of women in Michigan that $600 was chump change.

> "You're getting $600, what can you do with that? Not to be ungrateful or anything. But maybe it pays down a bill, but it doesn't pay down every bill every month. Barack's approach is that the short-term quick fix kinda stuff sounds good," she continued. "And it may even feel good that first month when you get that check. And then you go out and you buy a pair of earrings," she joked.

Seeing that Michelle Obama was standing there in $540 sneakers, nothing about this rant was amusing. After being called out in the press for her fancy feet, she would later dress down in J Crew and Black and White, threads for the commoner, as if that would make her high-handed attitude acceptable.

Americans are right to feel shafted. Obama told all us of that we would all need to have "skin in the game" in getting our economy back on track. To Goldman Sachs and Wells Fargo – who had both received stimulus checks – he demanded, "You can't get corporate jets, you can't go take a trip to Las Vegas or go down to the Super Bowl on the taxpayer's dime."

These comments didn't stop the President and First Lady from spending over $100,000 over two days for date night in New York City. Nor, did it curtail the President's golfing excursions. He played as much golf in nine months as President Bush did in two and a half years.

But the most undignified and the worst case of "let them eat cake" was our First Lady's trip to Spain with "40 of her closest friends" during the summer of 2010. This after the family had already taken seven vacations that year alone. Sigh. Perhaps this is a personal rub for me since I know in my own case and that of many of my friends that our children weren't in for a vacation that same summer. Like most Americans with serious skin in the game we played up the stay-cation as we awaited the fallout from higher taxes, job cuts, and rising costs of goods and services.

Our First Lady vacationing so lavishly and at such a bad time left most Americans   wondering, "Who are these people?" It was a big middle finger to the near double digit unemployment rate. It was a slap in the face to the speech Obama gave about spending time on the Florida coast to beef up their tourism. Such a startling degree of apathy and contempt for the mood of our country in harsh economic times was undignified considering our President is making it all worse as he piles on the laws, new stimulus spending, and tax increases across the board. It is safe to say that most Americans had plenty of skin in the game as it were.

Perhaps this quote by Michelle Obama says it all. "The truth is, most Americans don't want much," Obama said. "Folks don't want the whole pie. Most Americans feel blessed to thrive a little bit – but that's out of reach for them."

This is not at all our American truth. Our history is about striving for the very best life has to offer. Americans are not to be complacent with just enough to get by. We are the land of opportunity where anything as possible and should consider thriving about creating as many whole pies as we can.

Michelle Obama obviously does not see herself in this category of Americans who "can thrive on just a little bit" seeing as she has no problem flaunting just how many whole pies she has access to, with the help of our tax dollars to boot.

Now, don't misunderstand. I don't begrudge any person buying, wearing, or spending what they want on any good or service. And, I love to travel. What I mind, is someone else's idea of having skin in the game, is to use mine and not their own. I deeply resent being lectured to on how much skin is required when the one lecturing isn't even playing in the same league, let alone the same sport as I.

WHAT COULD HAVE BEEN

"...character and judgment. If you think about past Presidents, probably those two things along with vision are the most important aspects of a presidency. Do you know where you want to take the country? Do you have the judgment to figure out what's important and what's not? Do you have the character to withstand trials and tribulations and bounce back from setbacks?"

Barack Obama, Nov., 2007

Obama barreled in on Martin Luther King's theme "the fierce urgency of now." Though, as Obama's presidency picked up steam there were too many things rolling down like water and it wasn't freedom. He had a notion of where he wanted to take the country, but his directions overwhelmed us. When we stopped walking with him, he marched on full speed ahead without looking back. In taking on so many issues (most of them highly political and undesired), he stuffed America's cart to the brim. And, as Peggy Noonan so poignantly noted Americans began to fear that there were "too many people in the cart and not enough of us pulling it." Colin Powell who broke Republican allegiances to endorse Obama for President admitted, "He has lost some of the ability to connect that he had during the campaign. The American people feel that too many programs have come down. There are so many rocks in our knapsack now that we're having trouble carrying it. "

In the end, we were delusional to expect so much and so was the President in trying to be all things to all people. I can't help wonder what may have happened if our President would have just gone under the radar. What if he had avoided all the overexposure on the late night shows and daytime TV? What if he'd just slowed down and got focused on one core issue that Americans cared about: employment?

Though he felt frenzy over the economy and healthcare, "we just can't do nothing," I believe he could have done just that. He would have had a lot more success as a President in doing nothing. The truth is he hadn't done much anything before we elected him and it didn't stop him from winning us over and winning the election.

If he truly believed his words in 2004 about having faith in America and Americans, he would have let the American people work out the economy, mortgages, and health-care crisis. He would leave Arizona and its residents to handle their immigration issues.

He didn't have to go to Denmark chasing Olympic Gold. He didn't need to take over GM. He didn't need to go on *The View*. He didn't have to take on "don't ask, don't tell." He didn't need to take on health-care as quickly as he did in the midst of all this high water.

What if he had just decided to do what he did best? Go around the country each month and talk to the people and hear their stories and really get to know us and our hearts and give a good speech to work us up and inspire us to the challenge of creating our own jobs. And, what if he not only gave a speech about who we are, but what if he would not talk? Just listen.

Because had he listened, he would have found out that Americans just want to work, enjoy their family, and have their Government leave them alone. Most of us didn't want him to fail. We wanted him to succeed. We wanted our vision of success meaning that he would step aside and let us shine. We wanted him to succeed in our hopes and dreams, not his own personal agenda for bringing justice. That was the message he missed.

I suppose he was so high up on his pedestal he couldn't hear the very voices of those who put him up there. What he forgot way up there is that we needed a lot more of us and a lot less of him. For a time, we forgot that too.

ADDENDUM

From Tim Keller's *Counterfeit Gods*: The Signs of Political Idolatry

> After the last presidential election, my eighty-four year-old mother observed, 'It used to be that whoever was elected as your president, even if he wasn't the one you voted for, he was still your president.' That doesn't seem to be the case any longer. After the election there is now a significant number of people who see the incoming president lacking moral legitimacy. The increasing political polarization and bitterness we see in U.S. politics today is a sign that we have made political activism into a form of religion. Another sign of idolatry in our politics is that opponents are not considered to be simply mistaken but evil.

As President Obama's presidency comes to a close much of my heart and mind have been renewed and illuminated towards his two terms, his influence, and his reign. The words I wrote both sting and stun me. My hearty indulgence in my opinion and perceived omniscience catches my breath. I am glad to see how I admitted a love for Obama but I am dismayed by my lack of humility and pause in judging his heart, intentions, and purpose.

In fact, many of his comments that we, the right, conservatives, Republicans, blasted have come to make sense as a Christian. Among them, "You didn't build that." In the second campaign when Obama was running against Romney, a pedigreed, wealthy, Christian businessman, Obama made the pronouncement (credited to Elizabeth Warren), "you didn't build that." The right wing media and folks like myself went into a tizzy saying that Obama was disavowing hard work, sacrifice, and luring people into socialist ideas about wealth and equality.

I've since been humbled to see that he is exactly right. Whatever we have in might, riches, and opportunities is only by the grace of God. We build, have, and maintain nothing on our own. Much of who we are and our lot in life is completely outside our control: our race, gender, family background, where we were born, the region, the decade. We choose very little; we build even less, on our own.

Max Lucado offers a great analogy of this in *Outlive Your Life*. He plays basketball with his three year old nephew who loves anything bouncy and round. But the basketball is nearly as big as he is and the goal towers above him making it impossible for him to reach the basket never mind make a goal. After showing his nephew the granny toss, lifting him ever higher (about 3 times) towards the goal to give him a chance, his nephew finally drops the ball over the iron rim, all net whereby his nephew responds, "both fists into the air, 'All by myself! All by myself."

How much like Lucado's nephew we are when we see ourselves, our wealth, our liberty as self made and self sustaining. Where we refuse to acknowledge the grace and luck of our circumstances and blind ourselves to the travails and hardships of others who by no fault of their own but bearing many of our same talents, qualities, and work ethic, happen to be born into the wrong family, country, or race outside their doing.

The fact is if any of us have made it, no matter how hard we've worked or the decisions we've made, we are blessed and beyond the work of our own hands and talents. We were helped and often helped by the fact that many others are and have been historically disadvantaged.

During Obama's presidency, our country has been ravaged by the violent community killings of young black males, the suspicious death of a young black woman under police custody, and the vicious treatment of young black youths in suburbia. Many of these episodes caught on tape, we've now witnessed with our own eyes and have heard with our very own ears the cries and consequences of racial injustice that we previously denounced as "the race card."

Race has never been a tool or play that has worked in any black person's favor and now we understand that more than ever if we will have the heart to admit our stubborn lack of compassion and understanding.

It makes Obama's comment that the police acted "stupidly" with Professor Gates prophetic rather than rash. While running for Governor of Texas, I was immersed in researching the death penalty in Texas and the history and crimes of those who'd received it. It was staggering the numbers of poor, uneducated young black males (Hispanic next) in proportion to poor, uneducated white males who were incarcerated, and had died under a law that seemed to penalize circumstances and race as much as lawlessness.

The law, the system, and our society have been groomed to give up on certain lives. It seems we use the law as a way to relieve ourselves of our obligation to rehabilitate rather than punish and to ignore rather than answer to the economic devastation and years of racial denigration and disadvantage historical racism has birthed.

As pro-lifers, especially, we have partially and erroneously advocated for life much too narrowly and inconsistently. By concerning ourselves only with birth and ignoring the value of those same lives when they fall short in a system rigged and set coldly against them, we make being pro-life far too convenient. Why march and picket outside abortion clinics and fight so adamantly for laws to protect the unborn only to support killing them once they are full grown. You may say, the one life is innocent and the other is not. You may say, that person had his chance and chose to be a murderer. I would say to you be careful of seeing yourself as omniscient and meritorious, and seeing your "choices" and "chances" as completely within your control.

The entire criminal justice systems needs a rehabilitation where criminals can be reconnected with their humanity, gifts, and purpose in life. If someone resists transformation, then may he remain unfree but never unforgiven and never put to death except by the will of God.

As we made our way through Texas with our anti-poverty agenda for the nearly 19% of Texans living in poverty, it became clear that simply opening the door to "opportunity" and announcing the law made everyone equal is insufficient to beat centuries of laws and ideas that barbarically crushed the human spirit, economic opportunity, and erected barriers to progress, capital, and equality inflicted on a race of people.

It all seems so simple, black and white, when it isn't happening to us, our son, our family, our community, our neighbor. And, yet it already is. The point is if life matters, it matters at every stage and in every circumstance. We must protect the unborn and the living among us. If we continue to live in denial that the world is now everyone's oyster save for their personal choices, we invite more crime, more punishment, and more violence against ourselves, our communities and our world. And we're kidding ourselves if we think we can separate ourselves from the suffering just outside our door with our money, guns, politics, or religion. What we do or don't do unto to others, we cast upon ourselves.

Whatever it is we think we have built and whoever it is we have become, it is our calling to first give all glory and praise to the Lord and then to do for the least of these what we would have done to ourselves. To the fatherless, the widow, the beggar, are we their servants for thereby the grace of God do any of us go.

I feel compelled to share with you one final thing made aware to me on Obama and chosen leadership. The will of God always prevails. We vote but God anoints. He ultimately chooses our leader. When Obama was born, God knew he would become President of this country, at this time, at this place. God wasn't surprised that Obama edged Hillary out of the primary and beat Romney by huge margins in 2012.

For us to say, he should not be President and is unworthy of leading us is to say that our will and our knowledge is better than God's. Not only this, we are to submit to God's anointed leadership in the same way that David submitted to Saul. Though Saul had become a corrupt king, sought to kill David, and David knew he was next in line to become king, David respected God's anointing and will. Even having the right and the opportunity to kill Saul and take his rightful place, David humbled himself to God's anointed and will realizing that Saul was chosen by God and God alone was fit to judge him. Not only this, David humbled himself before Saul.

When Obama's tenure was put to me in this context, I realized just how prideful and arrogant I was to assume we can will the course of history by rallying a vote and raising up in anger and wrath against God's will.

So what would God have us do when we don't get the leader we want? When we don't get our way politically?

He'd have us realize that Government is not there to do what only the grace of God can no matter who is in office. He would have us remember that He cannot be here so he sent us to lead in our homes, our churches, in our communities to help the poor, love our neighbor, and look to him. All of these acts of service and love hold steadfast their effectiveness and power despite who sits in the oval office or occupies the seats of Congress.

"…the main problem in life is sin, and the only solution is God and his grace. The alternative to this view is to identify something besides sin as the main problem with the world and something besides God as the main remedy. That demonizes something that is not completely bad and makes an idol out of something that cannot be the ultimate good."
Tim Keller

SECTION II
Tea Parties

PATRIOTISM

Waking Up to Smell the Tea

What irony that the most famous community organizer of all time would be challenged by community organization. The Tea Party is now one of the largest and most viable power to the people movements of our generation. Exploring this irony further, it is surprising that Obama didn't find a way to utilize these efforts of community activism to his advantage. The Tea Party is essentially doing his life's work. Sadly, Obama would be the one to get most of the credit for fueling their movement and generating their power – against him.

The Tea Party had begun their efforts of protest and action well before Obama took office. Ron Paul's Tea Party '07 website raised $6 million dollars in just one day. Because it was Ron Paul receiving the support, I don't think most Americans were dialed in to the political potential of the Tea Party. I confess to thinking little of it at the time as well, even though, I was a Ron Paul supporter.

From where I sat, the Tea Party was mostly older Americans in middle America staging re-enactments of the original 1773 Boston Tea Party as a larger statement about Government overspending. It didn't occur to me that Barack Obama himself was the target of the Tea Party. Then as President Barack Obama got to work, he put the Tea Party in motion.

Americans were becoming more and more concerned on several fronts. The mortgage crisis had begun. Unemployment was at 7.7%. And, it was tougher to make ends meet. Despite this, Obama roared into office with a list of priorities that worsened these situations. He announced his plans to go full steam ahead with a $20 billion dollar health care plan even though word on the street was that most Americans- working Americans, business owning Americans, taxpaying Americans, didn't want it. He put in place multiple million dollar stimulus packages, bailed out General Motors, and continually blamed those earning over $250,000 for the shortfall of others less fortunate.

Americans had had enough, and what was worse, they had little respect for *this* man telling them what to do. Some credited this disrespect to prejudice against the first black President, some towards an uppity view of lower-income Americans. Mine was due to Obama's glaring lack of experience and his absence of common ground with majority of Americans.

Here we had a President who spent a great deal of his life in academia without a professional job in the private sector, who had never made payroll, had never had to make the tough decisions, or had to worry about the survival of a business. Yet, he would take over 1/6 of our nation's economy through health care. He would dictate to General Motors on restructuring their organization and what cars to manufacture.

Whatever the catalyst, it is clear that Obama and his current Democratic Congress have provided the Tea Party with ammunition and motivation for years to come, fueling a whole new political and social movement. Love them, hate them, The Tea Party isn't going anywhere as long as they continue a for the people by the people movement.

The Tea Party had its hiccups in the beginning: distasteful signs of Obama with a Hitler mustache; stubborn conspiracy theories about Obama's birth certificate. Tea Party members were slurred as tea baggers and dismissed as "When Hicks Attack." Even so, the Tea Party rose to indisputable power.

This grassroots organization resonated with many Americans who before wouldn't have had the courage to rally and protest on behalf of their conservative convictions. Power to the People! Despite the bias against them and without a central organization, they have prevailed into mainstream American politics and are a tour de force of political power.

What began as what the Tea Party is AGAINST: Barack Obama, BIG Government spending, Health Care Reform, or anything associated with the left is now a movement about what the Tea Party is FOR. And while the media and proponents of big Government have tried to mischaracterize the Tea Party as racist, radical, and mean spirited, it is today hardly any of those things.

Where great power is given, much is expected. The Tea Party must now tend to a nobler calling that edifies and rallies Americans toward unity and peace. How they do this and what battles they must choose and leave behind is as important as the progress we've made.

Because there are many similarities to the Tea Party Movement and the Civil Rights Movement of the 1960s it is important not to waste the lessons Martin Luther King, Jr. left us. In being a dominant political force, these conservative movers and shakers now have a responsibility to leave behind a legacy or hope and light. More than this, the Tea Party has an obligation to help lead this country away from the politically minded life structure and to God's word and will for our lives as his children, individuals, and as Americans.

CHAPTER FOUR

You're nobody in This Country Until Somebody Calls You a Racist

The Tea Party received a bad rap and perhaps at first, they earned it. In the beginning the images of the Tea Party movement came on too strong. Protests oozed with hot rage. Protesters brought signs with symbols of the Nazi regime. And what was with those signs of Obama depicted with the Hitler mustache and another with his face coming out of a donkey's you know what?

Those earlier days we'd rather put behind us like those pictures of us with bad teeth and hideous hair. Surely not everyone in the crowd had these unbearable signs, but as they say, one bad apple... The footage of the early months didn't lie and the combination of crass signs, shouts, and rage unsettled the average America. The Tea Party had a very good message, but in all that noise, the message was drowned out. They simply made too many people angry and uncomfortable.

The media declared a Tea Party fatwa. Gentle reports would refer to them as "angry protesters." The most derogatory term, 'tea baggers' caught on quickly. The classic, however, was redneck; since it in turn implies racism. For who is not racist, if not a redneck?

With these signs and disturbing images, the media was able to (and misguidedly so) dismiss the Tea Party as a fringe element. Similar to immigrants "living in the shadows", Tea Partiers were seen often, but rarely heard. Still, the Tea Party was more than who they were portrayed to be: the racist mob with nothing better to do than to bitch about Obama. As we came to learn though, anyone who had anything negative to say about President Obama was racist, logic or reason be darned.

Please welcome to Primetime, "the rednecks"

On MSNBC's "Countdown with Keith Olberman," actress Janeane Garofalo surmised, "let's be very honest about what this is about. It's not about bashing Democrats, it's not about taxes, they have no idea what the Boston Tea Party was about, they don't know their history at all. This is about hating a black man in the White House. This is racism straight up. That is nothing but a bunch of teabagging rednecks. And there is no way around that."

Political leaders were also quick to brand Tea Party members. Nancy Pelosi said that their disruption at town halls was "un-American." Barney Frank accused them of homophobic slurs.

The Tea Party could have used a little PR help. The Tea Party was spinning out in an image relations nightmare. They soon got a little help from the NAACP who stepped in hoping to do away with the Tea Party once and for all. How? Well, with what else but their tried and true, albeit tattered, race card. Problem was their tactic was easily and completely discredited.

Spitting Mad

The NAACP picked up where Janeane Garofalo, Nancy Pelosi and Barney Frank left off. What doesn't make sense is why? The NAACP had nothing to gain by labeling the Tea Party as racist, and the Tea Party had done nothing to provoke the NAACP. When, President and CEO Ben Jealous announced the NAACP's resolution to denounce the Tea Party as racist, it was one of those moments where I think most of us went, "Oh no, here we go again."

Not only did the NAACP shoot themselves in the foot, but they actually gave a boost to the Tea Party movement. Folks who had never been activists before were dismayed enough to reject the NAACP and accept the Tea Party. They figured the Tea Party could use more support from Americans like themselves – who they knew to be "fighting the good fight" out of obligation to values, not out of reaction to race. Inactive Americans who had agreed with the Tea Party, but were sitting out of the noise showed up to stick up for their beliefs.

With their conscience clear, folks got off the couch and joined the rallies because they weren't racist after all. And, as dull as the term "racist" had become, no one wanted to be called one. This claim only expanded the Tea Party's base, platform, and visibility.

At the same time, the New Black Panther Party was in the press for shouting vile racial slurs at whites, and breaking voter intimidation laws in the process. "I hate white people, all of them." "You want freedom, you gonna have to kill some cracker babies." These words spoken by New Black Panther leader Samir Shabazz makes the Tea Party chant "kill the bill" sound like a nursery rhyme. Shabazz's violent rants did more to prohibit the advancement of colored people.

"We believe in freedom of assembly and people raising their voices in a democracy. What we take issue with is the Tea Party's continued tolerance for bigotry and bigoted statements." This was the statement the NAACP released after passing their resolution. So in refusing to officially address and condemn the dangerous racism by the New Black Panther party, the NAACP's claims and their statement regarding the Tea Party hardly seemed credible. Moreover, their hypocrisy backfired.

These claims of racism without proof ultimately vindicated the Tea Party. In fact, the NAACP so victimized the Tea Party that the Tea Party looked unfairly targeted. They gained momentum and new activists of color, this author included, who refused to allow the NAACP to exploit race just so that they could go to bat for the Democrat party at America's expense.

The NAACP was unable to bamboozle and berate the Tea Party out of business. The resolution turned out to be a mass of empty calories. They seemed stuck in their own racist time machine seeking modern day relevance while working with an outdated manual. Here are three more logical reasons why the NAACP failed.

1. The Tea Party's agenda had nothing to do or say about race. No platform for or against anything having to do with minorities ever existed. The Tea Party's agenda never had anything to do with people of color, urban issues, or anything remotely pertaining to the advancement (or not) of any colored people. The Tea Party was boycotting BIG Government spending and laws being passed through BIG Congress.

2. Since the Tea Party was about reigning in Congressional power and spending, it's hard to imagine how they could be racist when Congress is 92% Caucasian. In the Senate is one black Senator out of a hundred. There are thirteen Jews, and one Hispanic. The House is only slightly more diverse. Of four hundred and thirty-five members there are thirty- one Jews and forty-two blacks, twenty-seven Hispanics, and three openly gay members. Out of 541 Congressional lawmakers, only 118 of them are a minority of some kind. And, if we count blacks only, that dwindles the number further to forty three or eight percent!

Does the NAACP mean to say a group of whites protesting BIG Government is racist even though the Congressional power they are protesting is over 90 percent white? Having a half-black President at the helm as the sole object of their retaliation is a wide stretch of logic that just doesn't cut it as racism.

1. Another thing that bit the hard cheese for the NAACP was that the members of the Tea Party had a backbone. The NAACP usually wins that game of chicken with big corporations, communities, and organizations, but the Tea Party did not retreat; they directly confronted the NAACP. Rather than tussle with an established civil rights group and bad press, organizations and businesses mostly decided it best concede to allegations of racism and find a way to "collaborate" with the NAACP. The Tea Party is different. As an individual and philosophical movement they had nothing to lose in standing up against the NAACP. The NAACP attacked people personally this time, an unboycottable (yes I made that word up) entity. It was clear that the race accusation was a decoy for spiteful retaliation to get back at Americans who disapproved of Obama and an overreaching Congress.

But "what about Representative Emanuel Cleaver being spat on?" I don't mean to sound like an episode of Seinfeld but there's a difference between projectile saliva intentionally directed at someone, or, the accidental spittle. Most of us reading this have been forced to reckon with spittle in one way or another. Either we've been spittled on, or, we have been the spittl*er*.

Even Mr. Cleaver conceded to his hometown media – in Kansas – that, "it could have been an accident." I didn't see that run on any major news network. Did you? Well, kudos to Cleaver for taking the high road.

Why the Tea Party is White

Given that ninety-percent of blacks voted for Obama and ninety-percent still support him, you would expect to see more whites than people of color at the Tea Party rallies. In general black backlash against Obama and Democrats doesn't exist. It would take all of Obama's black detractors to make a dent in the thousands of white protesters. Where black populations are miniscule the odds are even lower. Montana, Kansas, South Dakota, and Oregon, for example. To say that a sea of white protesters makes them or the movement racist means that simply marching while white is racist.

Since speaking at Tea Parties across the country, I've noticed that I'm often ignored by the media. I can think of one incident speaking in my hometown in Austin, Texas for a San Antonio Tea Party. It was quite tame, but still energetic. After a rousing speech, several attendees came up to thank me and to tell me how they enjoyed the speech. We hugged, laughed, and took pictures. News stations were there, some were a little late.

One station in particular was there the whole time, their reporter was sauntering all through the crowd looking left and right and talking to a few people hurriedly here and there. Not wanting to seem arrogant, I held back and thought she might want to talk with me since I was the premiere speaker, *and* black. So was she. Sensing this and knowing that she should, she finally made it over to me, but without the cameraman.

Reporter:	"Who are you?"
Lisa Fritsch	"I'm Lisa Fritsch,"
Reporter:	"Lisa, the speaker?"
LF:	"Yes, I was just speaking."
Reporter:	"Okay thanks."

And, off she trotted to the heavy set white couple holding a sign I couldn't make out. She wouldn't dare have any footage of an articulate, black, Tea Party speaker hugging and loving on a bunch of "rednecks" making the local news, 'not on her watch.'

And the beat goes on. . .

The Colors that Matter: Speech Excerpt

I have to tell you when I look out into the crowd at all of us; I don't see black, white, and brown. I see RED, WHITE, and BLUE!!!!

Standing in these colors, we are unmoved by the tactics of divisiveness through race, social status, and politics. Because we are motivated by the fight for our individual rights, not the motivation of one group over another, we will succeed in the individual greatness of each other that lends a collective good. We are not here merely because of our strength in numbers. We are here because we know we are a masterful quilt with patches of genius pieced throughout. With colors of suffering shared among us. And threaded together by common stories of eventual triumph and opportunity. We are here because we are individually responsible for this great country. We will not blend into a mass of populist ideas and platforms. But we will stand out in defense of each and every one of our individual freedoms. For our strength today is in asserting our rights to our individuality and our duty to protect the sovereignty in these great lands.

That's the spirit of the Tea Party not just in black and white, but in red, white, and blue!

CHAPTER FIVE

"Get Back Honky Cat"

Who You Callin' a redneck? Not that there's anything wrong with that...

Growing up my grandfather explained to me that the term redneck came about from men who worked outside on the farm all day. They usually wore coveralls to protect themselves from the sun, but because their shirt collar left their neck exposed, it would turn red, hence the term redneck. Hearing this explanation, I thought, 'what is wrong with someone being a "redneck," seeing as they got that way from hard work'?

I'm not convinced that Tea Party participants were ever really a bunch of rednecks, even though the media would have us believe that. What I saw when I looked into the eyes of the protesters were everyday people who were fed up with Government. Though to the elite media and political establishment a "redneck" might be anyone living south of Boston without the Ivy growing around their collars.

This stunning portrayal of anti-Government activists as minor players from an uneducated and ignorant class revealed a bifurcation in our country that has gone hidden for some time. It goes well beyond the blue state, red state thing. This split is not even about a division of values and core beliefs. It all boils down to the political and media elite thinking they are high above the majority of the American electorate. It reveals their ignorance about just who comprises the middle class are, what true intellect is, and in whom it can reside. They can't begin to know what an ordinary American looks like let alone what gets their heart racing.

The Tea Party created a 'you people' moment. The redneck factor was less about geographical and educational bias and more a frustration that the elites had to deal with these people. Suddenly, all these little people that Obama and his administration were supposedly fighting for started coming out against him and his policies. Awkward.

An angry mob of wealthy elitist, conservative Republicans not wanting to "pay their fair share" would have been an easy voice to dismiss. However, the Tea Partiers were and are those ordinary Americans from all over who the Government and the Obama administration expected to be seen and not heard.

The egalitarian philosophy wouldn't cut it as Obama and the media would try and paint healthcare with a brush of fairness and equality. The rednecks were smarter than they looked. Before Obama and BIG Government spoke to this "middle class" as a mythical and enduring group; they were this entity of Americans who were neither here nor there, in the middle. We all talk about the "middle class" but does anyone really know who they are? We do now. Turns out, the rednecks are the middle class – that group that Obama was working so hard to protect and defend with all his policies.

A 2010 Gallup poll revealed that nearly 43% of Tea Partiers identified themselves as independents. And, while the going thought was that Tea Partiers were the uneducated masses, nearly 37% had a college degree. Not only are they not rednecks, not that there is anything wrong with that; they are the blue and white collar working class – the prized demographic of the Democratic Party.

Fed Up

On every plane it seemed BIG Government was sticking it to the big, middle, and little guy infringing on their constituents liberties and life choices. The smokers got the baton first. After all, everyone knows that smoking is bad for you and your neighbor, and second-hand smoke is just as bad for the non-smoker. Next thing you know, smoking was banned from restaurants AND bars. (Don't people go to bars to smoke?) Then smokers couldn't smoke directly outside of any venue. And as unbelievable as it is, some states contend that smokers shouldn't smoke in rented apartments. "Too bad for them thought most of us non-smokers. We skipped merrily along to Krispy Kreme thinking how we could never understand inhaling all that disgusting smoke in the first place."

Why didn't us porkies see that we were next? We are in a war on obesity after all. Not that second hand fat is contagious, but if you are fat, we all end up paying in the long run especially now with Universal Health Care. We have a vested interest in each other's health; therefore, fat is also contagious the more you think about it. And, think of the kids. Trans-fats and those of us who look to them in fragile times were put on notice. Trans fats were bad and so were the people who ate them. Surveys were done to show that fat people were less productive and intelligent. Fat kids went to jail. Skinny kids made it to Harvard. New York was the first state to ban the fatty fats from restaurants and soon after they plunged into salt prohibition.

States were going too far in an effort to do what was best for us. Higher taxes were everywhere, notwithstanding the emerging blow healthcare reform. Tolls, airport fees and surcharges, hotel's extra city and state taxes and fees. Everywhere we went, it was fee this and tax that. Besides one's state and federal taxes an average working person was hit with about six different taxes each day. Surely, this can't all be about paying our fair share for decent roads and civilized society. There wasn't anything fair about paying one's "fair share" – unless you are among the 40% of Americans who pay no income and Federal taxes at all. This is not a picture of home of free or the brave.

Americans all over the country were paying attention to these town hall and rallies, but Congress wasn't listening. Suddenly, a lot of what the Tea Party said made sense. And, wasn't that Martha from bunko night? Eyes began opening to just how severely their rights were being flushed down the toilet, one stimulus, one bailout, and one social program after another.

Because it wasn't just Obama, these movements for the people where not just happening in the Southern, "redneck" states. New Yorker's were FED up. Chicagoans, FED up. Texans, FED up. Even folks in the most liberal lands like Seattle, Oregon, New Hampshire, Massachusetts, and Delaware were FED UP!

Those most fed up started fleeing heavy taxing states like New York and California for easier places to live and pursue happiness like Texas, Florida, and Georgia. Even though they would flee to these states (one attraction for Texas and Florida is the lack of state income tax), they recognized that they shouldn't have to. This Tea Party thing was on to something and well, if it is a bunch of rednecks, the heck with it. Where do I sign up? They were FIRED up!

Fired Up

Was the Tea Party started as a simple exercise in recognizing the rebellion of the Boston Tea Party in 1773 to parallel today's frustration at growing Government spending? Was it the famous Santelli rant on CNBC's "Squawkbox" that got replayed several hundred times all over talk waves and television news programs where he decried 'loser's mortgages," and that there were too many people drinking the water and not carrying it? Yes, Santelli struck a chord with fed-up Americans over Government spending, but he also mentioned that Chicago needed a Tea Party rally. And they got one.

Several theories float around on how and why the Tea Party really got started. It isn't exactly clear at what date the Party began organizing and coming together and exactly what prompted it, but what is clear is that they are here to stay and they have struck a nerve.

I can recall as early as 2007 during the Ron Paul campaign, which I supported, his having an affiliation with the Tea Party. With a Tea Party '07 website, Paul was raised more than $6 million dollars in one day. And this is before the Tea Party's own political candidates started to rock the political world.

Why the Tea Party began seems connected the disappearing notion of the American Dream. "Don't Tread on Me," a slogan adopted by the Tea Party a bit later speaks to this. Americans started to fear the idea of Government inception in every facet of their lives without any benefit to the majority of Americans. In fact, Americans and our country in general were worse off. In areas where we were previously dominant, we were sliding drastically compared to our contemporaries around the world. We ranked much lower in college graduates, math and science, GDP. Areas where we had the greatest growth were not good: obesity, heart disease, national debt, out of wedlock birth. This was the first generation where it appeared that children could not expect to do better than their parents. Obama's healthcare bill attested to this as he and Congress made it so that children could stay on their parent's plan until they were twenty-six years old! This was not what it meant to be an American. And there wasn't a racist sentiment in this fear whatsoever.

It was clear that the Tea Party meant business. By the end of 2009 The Tea Party was not simply about Obama. He may have been a symbol of their rage, but he would not be the only one. From here on out, all politicians would be on notice. For it wasn't just that the Tea Party was gaining momentum, but also that their momentum was that of the will of the people. Their power was an expression of conservative values.

Still, the Tea Party wouldn't get really cranked up until Barack Obama made it clear that despite a falling economy and collapsing mortgage industry, he was heavy on Universal Health Care with a side of pork. This was the final straw. Was it final because he was the first black President with the audacity to tell Americans to shut up and take it? For me it is too complicated to simply say no, it isn't. Would the Tea Party have been less agile if Hillary Clinton were President? I don't know. Hillary Clinton didn't campaign with posters of her face floating around in dulled colors of red and blue that seemed to ominously remind folks of Castro and communism.

So I do think Obama himself played a role in igniting the Tea Party so fiercely not because he was black, but because he was deaf. For someone who ran a campaign for the people, he was not listening. The Tea Party decided they would speak louder and haven't shut up since.

As I followed news and the Tea Party Movement from 2008-2009, it was too intense for me. I was put off by the signs: there was Obama in the Hitler mustache and the one where he is the tail end of a donkey. I mentioned this on a radio program in 2010 and the host quickly corrected me that those signs had nothing to do with the Tea Party. They were the manifestation of some other organization. Nevertheless, those signs were on constant display at most rallies. To me they were a crass display of disrespect, not only for our President, but for the proper way to dissent. Just as I'd never agreed with portrayals of Bush as a chimp, I considered those posters out of line.

I wasn't put off by the media's description of the Tea Party as the low class uneducated masses. Not at all. But I did think the mood too filled with rage and militancy. The Tea Party did come off as an angry mob, no matter what some activists and members will tell you now. And, because their attention seemed singularly focused on Obama, race was also a factor. I was uncomfortable with being labeled.

My role as a Tea Party speaker and supporter happened gradually as I saw a calling to be a voice in the party I wasn't hearing. Because there is no central helm and leadership of the Tea Party, it is an authentic way towards individual expression of conservative values. That is what is so effective and unique about the movement.

As a conservative talk show host, I would often say on the air that I agreed with their platform of smaller Government, the Constitution and fiscal discipline, but I would admonish the signs and the rhetoric. For a year, I politely declined invitations to speak at rallies and meetings because I did not agree with the tactics. I would never want my children to see my face associated with groups treating our President distastefully.

After appearing on "Glenn Beck," offers escalated to several invitations a week. Initially, I turned them all down. I did not want to be part of what I also perceived as a fringe movement that was only about getting back at President Obama for failing the country. I felt Obama brought a new set of problems, but I also felt that our issues as who we are as Americans and the direction we were headed as a country were larger than him. Besides, I didn't want anything to do with those signs.

I was naïve at the time about the visibility being on Glenn Beck would bring. I had heard of Glenn Beck, but I was not a core follower. I had no idea that he was the "conservative Oprah." After appearing on the show and saying my piece, I received several hundred emails and letters about my remarks, from Tea Party supporters and detractors. I suppose from my comments many just assumed I was a Tea Partier. Some were kind and invited me to dinner and to speak and so on:

"If you ever consider moving to this area please let me know...I need a good neighbor."

Others were less impressed:

> "Let's all celebrate R. Reagan who created the infamous welfare queen, And you, even with your straight haired wig would have been mistaken for a welfare gal and treated accordingly by the police, the store owner, your teachers, etc. You know what I'm talking about. . . Do you not think race is not a factor in the Tea Party movement? Beck is using you... I hope it pays well."

And, some prompted me to think further about my role in speaking out on social issues in a more meaningful way. More than the letters of kind invitation, or disgust at my nerve and point of view, people shared their own stories and called me to a higher level talking of my being a "great American." They urged me to keep "fighting the good fight." People said they would pray for me and my family. I responded to everyone who wrote me during that first appearance, and in some letters formed a spiritual connection that held me accountable to my words. One such letter was from Pastor Wil Moore:

> "My comment to you was that I've read your life growing up in Tyler and understand how you feel as an American, however with nothing said I was disturbed by your recent appearance on the Glenn Beck show. Not that I have any problem with Glenn Beck. But what disturbed and bothered me was when I viewed the telecast all that went through my mind and heart was sadness for my people. First I would have much preferred to have seen this in a light with you hosting the show. When will we as a people stop

allowing others to pimp us. Offering us our 15 minutes of fame. I was somewhat embarrassed because as history has continually shown we're always on the receiving end of things. My grandfather and mother new and marched with King personally and from the stories that I've gotten from them, blacks in America on both sides still miss the mark and the heart of the message. This is very sad. Mind you I'm not a conservative nor am I a liberal. Being an historian and English teacher I understand both by true definition. And in understanding the true sense of the meaning I chose not to live my life according to those standards but according to the standards of kingdomship in God. You made a statement and I quote "I know as a Christian that feelings of worthlessness, defeatism, and victimization, do not come from God. And as his children he has for us a life full of unique purpose and divine intention." I love this and I pray that this is the very fabric of your being. I am also a retired Army Vet and there was so much controversy surrounding the deployment of 40,000 troops to Afghanistan. I've been and the decision I promise you is not an easy one. While I understand your struggle with him dithering, I also understand his dilemma. Again I say I've been there and I have a son still there. Comments are easily made behind a mic and a desk in Washington good or bad. Mind you I am not a supporter of many of the President's policies and I do pray that he falls in love with us as well, but in closing I would encourage you to mind the speaking engagements you take, the words you say, the manner in which you say them. Please don't stop being a no-nonsense radio talk show host, but remember that the scriptures state that in Romans 13:1 "Everyone must submit himself to the Governmental authorities, for there is no authority

97

except that which God has established. The
authorities that exist have been established by God."
The big picture Lisa is that as the old folks use to say
"A new broom (Barack Obama) knows how to sweep
the floor but an old broom (God) knows where to find
the dirt. Love you Sis. And don't let anyone ever
prostitute your gift again."

I am one who believes everything happens for a
reason. That we all have our time and place to meet our
God-given destiny. Being on Glenn Beck's show was one
such moment for me among others.

Of course, Obama was **the one** who ignited the Tea
Party and got their kettle whistling. His chosenness was to
bring us back to our senses just as our chosenness it to do
the same. Where Obama failed in joining our Americanism,
he succeeding in making us recognize our own. Before he
was elected, our mirrors were misdirected. Had it not been
for his petulant and adamant ways, record breaking
spending, and out of control deficit, the Tea Party may have
never galvanized so fiercely.

What if Obama's race ignited this force? I'll bet it
didn't. Still, if we want to address Obama's race, we can
only say that it was an asset during the election. If his race
played a factor in compelling the Tea Party, it would have
stemmed from great disappointment rather than hatred or
disgust. Was it because Obama was labeled a socialist?
Actually, it seems Obama's ideology was more dangerous
than socialism. Socialist or not, we were headed towards a
road that was clearly un-American; we needed a corrective
course. I think more than his race or our socialist
suspicions, he came across as un-American. That fired up
the Tea Party.

The NAACP resolution was the final straw. I too was
fed up with being told that I was a sell-out to my race
because I refused to agonize over being black and conspire

race and discrimination theories. I was fed up with being called an Uncle Tom for calling the liberal agenda out for its destructive and diabolical agenda. I was fed up always hearing the discussion on racism and rejection without addressing the conservative antidote to combat their pervasiveness. I was fed up with having to defend why I'm a child of God first, and an American second, and black finally. And, I was fed up paying more than my fair share, but also being lectured that I didn't have enough skin in the game.

I wanted to be part of correcting the course. I wanted to be above the noise and be more than the rumble of anger and rage. I was FIRED UP!

Tea Party Speech Excerpt

We find ourselves in the midst of our own inconvenient truth. The truth today is our Government has taken advantage of us. For too long we have been comfortable, drunk on our former successes, and complacent with our livelihood and now we have been stirred awake by the jarring feeling of insecurity and uneasiness. That uneasiness comes from the fact that while we've been asleep, our Government has fed on our passivity. Our Government, as my big mama used to say has "gotten too big for its britches."

We've awakened to find our place in this great land diminished and decaying. But thankfully, we have been jolted awake by that deep rooted knowledge of Americanism. Just in time with this rally, this party, and this movement is a testimony that we will never fall asleep at the wheel again.

We are not here because of one man. We are not here because of one law. We are not here because of one single event. A culmination of changes and false hopes have told our souls we must be here. We are here because we are the ones we have been waiting for.

We are here because we can no longer sit idly by as our Government spends our children into submission. We will not go to the back of the bus of liberty as our Government taxes us into serfdom and slavery.

Now they say in Texas, it ain't braggin' if it's true, so it is with great pride that I say, I'm proud to be an American and I want our children to be proud to be Americans...We can no longer afford to turn a blind eye while our textbooks are rewritten and contrived to distort our history so that our children are no longer proud to stand up and say, I love my country, but are instead taught to ignore America's greatness and special place in the world.

And finally, we will no longer cool our heels and wait for the one, or anyone, to tell us who we are and who we ought to be, or what we cannot have, do, eat, think, say, and drive! For no one can define us but God who has provided us free will in which to reign over ourselves individually in liberty. This is the Tea Party.

And because our rights and our identity come from God - not man - we have become alarmed at a Government that seeks to replace GOD. We are distrustful of a Government that disrespects who we are as individuals. We desire God's will for us, not the will of our Government. As the Government moves to control all corners of our life, we say STOP! We want our life back and the God given dignities of life: the dignity of prayer, self-control, hard work, sacrifice, family, duty, honor, and courage. We are the Tea Party!

We are here to attest to the freedom and land of opportunity and equality for all of which we are entitled. We have much we can learn from Civil Rights struggles not much unlike ours today that have gone before. Dr. King, our greatest mentor in the struggle for freedom and civil rights said it best, "we know from painful experience that freedom is never voluntarily given by the oppressor; it must be demanded by the oppressed." So we know it will not be easy to reclaim the freedoms we have lost, but still, we will demand it. We will refuse to be oppressed. We are here to restore our faith in America and therefore ourselves. We are the Tea Party and inheritors of the land of the free and proud to live in the home of the brave.

ADDENDUM

Turns out that Pastor Moore saw more clearly through his television what I could not those moments on Fox News Channel. So much of what he mentioned in his note to me was taken to heart. And, so much proved true during the gubernatorial campaign. He was right that I'd allowed my gift to be prostituted by the media and the Republican status quo. He was right that I should be selective about where and how I use my voice.

Stepping from behind the microphone, off the stage and into the arena, I exposed myself to the difference in talking one's values and the integrity/pain/cost of living them.

I find myself embarrassed but forced to admit that the notion of a black conservative is more than a little foolish when one considers what it means buying acceptance by denying an experience and the effects of shame and race. When I ran, I saw how clearly black conservatives are used for the expediency of a false premise. After my eyes were opened and I took off all those labels that I no longer defined me, I experienced the backlash from friends and strangers alike against someone who couldn't be their black ally in promoting the fantasy that white privilege and racial harm no longer exist.

One person wrote, "I thought you were for the forgiveness and moving on of that past." Surely I still am, but I am also for acknowledging that the injustice of the past did not die with those who lynched black people. With forgiveness must come retribution, and respect for the reality that racism has been a harm to the reality of black lives today. I read it best in the book, *Americanah*. "...lots of white folks are still inheriting money that their families made a hundred years ago. So if that legacy lives, why not the legacy of slavery?"

I will forever believe love and the power to forgive that love wills us can conquer all things. But to affirm people in the falsehood that racism can be cured simply by the will, prayers, and self-reliant fortitude of African-Americans alone is too much to ask. It is a collective call to justice, breaking systems and barriers down, healing and forgiveness for humanity's sake.

Most in right wing politics and media want the same thing that leaders on the left side of politics and media want: more money, more viewers, more power, and to protect "their right" to be the one telling and deciding for everyone else what is best.

Depending on your own political leanings, you many think that I simply sound cynical and bitter now. My leftist friends and adversaries thought I was self-loathing and naive when this came out. You may both be right. I can only tell you that today I am empowered and informed in my views. And with this new information, my skepticism goes to both sides, my devotion to neither.

CHAPTER SIX

Turning Protest into Power

Power to the People

'Power to the People' isn't always pretty. But when built on the truth by discovery, these movements are powerful and effective beyond measure. The Tea Party's power to the people movement has galvanized millions of Americans and is changing the political landscape. It is a rags to riches tale of ascent to political influence and power despite character attacks and the absence of "leadership." How did this happen?

It wasn't just Obama; that gives him way too much credit and dismisses the value of sacrifice and understanding the movement has generated. A reactionary movement eventually teeters out and/or becomes overwhelmed at the thought of growth and organization. It couldn't just be about the laws, Congress, and the tax burden befalling us. All of these things are relevant but paint an incomplete picture of the Tea Party's trajectory.

The struggle in living with a fracturing economy, a morally decaying civilization, and a ballooning debt to the trillions of dollars has triggered an awakening of humanity. The people, their humanness, are now driving the power of politics. The people are on a path to discovery and therefore; independence. Independence is power – and this is how the Tea Party was able to transform protests into power and therefore, politics.

It is very similar to the Civil Rights Movement of the 1960s. The people, not just Martin Luther King, Jr, the church, or the Government made a discovery. They discovered the truth: they were equal in the eyes of God and therefore the Government could not make laws that spoke otherwise. And while they had sat politely and tolerated it up to a point, the truth was bursting free in their souls. An awakened soul wouldn't allow them to the luxury of passivity any longer. That truth translated into power of the people. Black people in the 1960s turned their protest into power and politics accomplishing more than I imagine they even sought to do. But even as their work was not yet done, we'll see how the Tea Party still has more work to do.

The truth for the people of the Tea Party is that our souls will not allow us to rest. Just as the soul of the black community was not at rest then, so too do our souls toss and turn. We know there is a better America yearning to break free of this cycle of Government dependence. We know that Americans can do better than just wait on checks on the 1st and the 15th.

We know that we have the ingenuity to build, create, and manufacture right here in our own lands. Every time we shop at Target and fill up our carts with products all "Made in China" it burns us in a place we don't see, but we can feel. We are better than this. We can DO better than this.

What we want is for our politicians, our leaders, and our neighbors to recognize this too. When we try to tell them, they don't hear us because they see the anger and frustration without understanding that inside our hearts are weeping. Instead of helping us, they tried to contain us and sit us down. We are continually talking but not communicating. Still, if only they would have tried to listen.

A friend and I were talking one morning about politics, hence the Tea Party when she made a sharp observation, "you know, Obama should embrace the Tea Party, what as a former acclaimed community organizer?" We continued to discuss the irony in the movement considering Obama's celebrated status as a community organizer. It got me thinking, what if Obama had found a way to work with this grass roots community structure. That profound notion could have completely changed the course of the Tea Party and perhaps the people's power. (Maybe David Axelrod isn't an evil genius after all.)

The Tea Party is simply an assembly of fed up individuals. You cannot attack individuals as a unit. In order for the Tea Party's opponents to neutralize the Tea Party, they needed to first understand them. And, to understand them, you would need to understand and acknowledge the power of the individual. (Sadly, however, this is a concept the left doesn't buy into on any level.) They never bothered to do that. Their tactic was to ignore and detach themselves from the people.

Since no one would listen to them, these ordinary Americans changed and influenced Washington politics the "hard, easy" way. Local citizens organized rallies, rented buses to marches, got out the vote with neighborhood drives, gathered in homes, held meetings to study our history and our Constitution, and took up their Saturdays to gather at Capitols and parks. Without any help or recognition from the top, they changed the course in Washington from the bottom up. How can one not be in awe over this devout expression of the people's voice and power? This is community organizing and activism in its most organic and authentic form.

Give Obama credit for igniting the Tea Party if you want. If you do, you can say this has been his most effective and groundbreaking community organizing campaign to date. Since Obama's political career began as a community organizer, it's a shame that he does not marvel at the Tea Party's rise to prominence with admiration and praise. Better yet, he should have immersed himself in his people, if not to work with them, at least to listen to what they were really trying to say.

What would have been a marvelous use of his skills –
not to mention a brilliant way to take the edge off of their
swords – Obama's insight into community organization
should have been an asset to his administration and
Congress. Instead Obama aligned himself with the political
trinity – Congress, the media, and Obama – and
underestimated this grassroots effort. Their attacks
cemented the convictions of the Tea Party against the
Government.

It wasn't until Scott Brown defeated Martha Coakley
for Ted Kennedy's senate seat with a large helping of Tea
Party votes, that the political trinity took notice. Still, they
were unphased and claimed that Scott Brown should be
prepared to join them in the status quo.

By the time the political trinity truly grasped the
scope of the Tea Party's potential and power, it was way
too late. The political trinity scrambled to fight back, but
they were miles behind the movement. The Tea Party had
already pushed Sharon Angle in Nevada giving Harry Reid
an embarrassing run for his money. Sarah Palin lined up
"Mama Grizzlies" and a few papas too, and Christine
O'Donnell in Delaware came out of no-where to best a
long-time Republican shoo-in Mike Castle.

Because they don't get the concept of "power to the
people," the power of the Tea Party continues to elude the
Washington establishment and the media.   They still
wonder, "How does this power function?"   "Where does
the power come from?"   "How does it keep running?"
"How does it translate into politics?" And, "why is it
effective?" "What's next?"

The power comes from knowledge of our rights and
our founding principles. The fruits of liberty call for living
the truth and making sacrifices. Living the truth and
making sacrifices lends power. The power is derived from
individual discovery and courage. The power is
authenticated and runs on the apathy of the adversary, or

the adversary's rebuttal to change. But since "you can't change what you don't acknowledge" (Dr. Phil) – as in the political trinity's refusal to acknowledge their true role in the Tea Party's upheaval – the Tea Party's movement and power grew to greater heights. This power is effective in politics because it really isn't political at all. The revolt is about values and morality. The longevity and what's next depends on the movement's continued recognition – and the adversary's concession – that their power comes from the people. And, as the people continue to sacrifice and diligently seek and discover themselves in the right places – the Bible and the Constitution – their reign can live on indeterminately.

The People's Message

The Tea Party's power is that they are a movement that comes from the people. With their recent political power, they have been called out to explain themselves. But how? There is no explaining to be done. The Tea Party is only as strong as each person who supports the movement with the courage to vote their values.

The worst thing that the party can do would be to adopt a structure and an organized platform. This would deflate the energy and power of the people; thereby diminishing the movement and its results. I imagine it is going to be tempting for a few distinguished talking heads: Dick Army, FreedomWorks, Tea Party Express, who are largely credited with building the party's power, to resist organizational structure. I believe that the minute, the Tea Party is a third party of any kind, the party will be over.

The Tea Party has accomplished many goals to attain power and have a voice in the political mainstream. And, they have worked hard for it. Now, they must face a new challenge and that is to stay on message.

Keeping It Real

The Tea Party has obviously hit a nerve in the political bedrock. First Karl Rove got in a tizzy over O'Donnell besting the establishment Republican in Delaware. Rove blamed Tea Party candidate O'Donnell for a failure before it occurred. Then Bill Clinton accused the Tea Party of wanting to weaken the Government and leave big business unsupervised – maybe Clinton supposes that big business might go wild making profits, manufacturing new ideas, and HIRING people without the Government there to regulate and tax them to death. A few days later, President Obama wants the Tea Party's expertise in cutting the national debt and creating jobs.

The Tea Party would be wise to avoid these distraction tactics put on by triangulating politicians. There are very simple ways to answer all these critics, particularly Clinton and Obama, without taking the bait of diluting the will of the people.

To answer Mr. Clinton the Tea Party members certainly want a strong Government. Tea Partiers want a Government strong enough to secure our borders, build up our military, and govern based on the Constitution. Where our Government has atrophied and gone astray, the Tea Party would like it to work the muscles of defense and fiscal responsibility again. As it relates to big business, I think most members of the Tea Party are willing to take the risk of big business gone wild.

The Tea Party has no beef with the private sector as Clinton would try and have us believe. Just who does Clinton think the private sector is? It isn't just Wall Street and big automobile manufacturers and their mogul friends like Warren Buffett and George Soros.

The private sector is your neighborhood eatery just barely scraping by charging for extra salad dressing these days and to-go containers. They are your stay at home moms working Mary Kay or running an online business part-time. The private sector is full of Americans struggling to find a business to hire them. The private sector is full of Americans with great ideas hoping to turn a small business *into* a BIG business someday. Besides this, the Government is doing a fine job all on their own in revolting against the private sector.

In an effort to deflect attention from his responsibility, President Obama was next to breathe down the Tea Party's neck. "The challenge, I think, for the Tea Party movement is to identify specifically, what would you do?" "It's not enough just to say, 'Get control of spending.' I think it's important for you to say, 'You know, I'm willing to cut veterans' benefits,' or, 'I'm willing to cut Medicare or Social Security benefits,' or, 'I'm willing to see these taxes go up.'"

An Obama supporter spoke eloquently for everyone at an Obama town hall last fall when she wondered if she was returning to the days of beans and weenies. "Is this our new reality?" She asked quizzically, and pleaded for him to answer this most of all. Of course, he did not. Obama rambled diffusely about having two kids to put through college and how the Government would make it easier for her and others to borrow money to achieve this goal. The problem in this answer is twofold: borrowing money and getting student loan grants for the Government is yet, another overreaching program, spending money out of our very own thinning pockets. Secondly, this lady didn't stand up and ask President Obama for a hand-out. She wanted to know how she would be able to have control over her own destiny – pocketbook – again.

The Tea Party would be wise to sit tight on responding to challenges Clinton and Obama posed. The Tea Party is a philosophical movement designed to restore us back to our small Government roots.

Tellin' It like It Is

What is so effective about the Tea Party and so very frustrating for the good ol' boy network of Democrats and Republicans is that the Tea Party is truly a movement of the people. Without a leader to call by name, or a platform to criticize based on rhetoric, the Tea Party leaves the Democrats and Republicans flat footed in their triangulation efforts. The minute the Tea Party responds to these notions by changing their fundamental platform, they will fall into a political trap of petty finger pointing in place of action.

Obviously the Tea Party is close to accomplishing goals neither Democrats nor Republicans thought possible: raising money and getting seats. The Tea Party activists and supporters are doing just what they need to do: call Americans back to the safety of our Constitution and shine a light on the Government's overreaching and over spending hand.

Tea Party Speech Excerpt

Where this Tea Party began out of frustration of a bloated Government and a cup runneth over in debt let it carry forth as a restoration. The truth is that we must restore America and our brothers and sisters to humanity so that we can regain our faith in this country again. The truth is that we are not simply here to elevate one political party or the other, but we are here to lift up and encourage one another to be the greatest version of themselves in the eyes of our Creator. This greatness cannot come from our political leaders. It is inherently placed in us by our Creator and it is a simple philosophy of responsibility.

Therefore it is obvious that we must move toward restoration and a renewed faith in ourselves and our country. As we fight for our freedoms and our humanity, we will fight peacefully, with love in our hearts and whispers of gratitude and thanksgiving rolling off our tongues. This restoration is less about candidates than about ourselves, striving to bring forth the bounty of fruits in the seeds planted in us by our Creator. And so as it is and as we have learned that there can be no lasting victory and humanity without God, we ask that God lead us in our gathering, and in our thoughts, and in our actions with ourselves and each other. For if God is with us who then can prevail against us. So let us not stand here today as Republicans, Democrats, Libertarians, rich, poor, but let's really get back to basics. Let's return to our basic selves – as children of God seeking our God given rights in this country to life, liberty, and the pursuit of happiness. Let every politician, in every office, in every state; regardless of party hear our voice. Government will not be our God.

By taking responsibility for ourselves and our families we restore our faith in each other which is the key to restoring our faith in America. Our faith was never lost, only buried in the fog of external expectation. Should we renew our faith in the will and purpose of God, there we will find our redemption and our reward.

And our reward will be that we are able to stand firm and say with conviction and warm hearts the words of the founders: that we hold these truths to be self-evident, that all men are created equal, that they are endowed by their Creator with certain unalienable Rights, that among these are Life, Liberty and the pursuit of Happiness. That to secure these rights, Governments are instituted among Men, deriving their just powers from the consent of the governed. With a firm reliance on the protection of divine Providence, we mutually pledge to each other our Lives, our Fortunes and our sacred Honor.

CHAPTER SEVEN

The Tea Party is Relevant Now What

"I am not interested in power for power's sake, but I'm interested in power that is moral, that is right and that is good."

Martin Luther King, Jr.

Everything does happen for a reason. We are here in this point in time for a reason. Obama was here and elected to show us the way towards our greater purpose. We've come to a crucial breaking point where we know we can no longer advance in the direction we're headed. To whom then shall we go? As our ancestors have struggled and prevailed against harsh economic times, unjust civil time in history, and wars and battles, here we are today, taking our place in history as we fight our own fight back towards our values and our humanity. We are not the first generation to be called to restore America to what is right and true. History is on our side.

I've remarked often how the Tea Party Movement reminds me a great deal of the Civil Rights Movement. Not because we are fighting for rights, rather in the way that we must carry ourselves and be accountable to one another. There is so much to be learned from the Civil Rights movement of the past.

What we are fighting for is only as noble as the means to our victory and the image of love we project. As we call ourselves and each other to stand up, it's an imperative that we stand with God, honor, and humanity. Luckily, we don't have to start from scratch. It is as if Martin Luther King left us a blueprint for our own struggle.

All quotes in this chapter are from Dr. King. He wrote freedom's manifesto. In it is a model for excellence, grace, God's hand, and victory.

Like the Civil Rights Movement itself, the work of the Tea Party must be based on Faith. The Tea Party must follow in the Civil Rights Movement's principles of nonviolence and civil disobedience. In the words of Dr. King "We must forever conduct our struggle on the high plane of dignity and discipline," To achieve continued success the Tea Party must apply important lessons from the Civil Rights movement that came before:

- Follow the path of **Light**
- Embrace **Our Neighbors** in the struggle
- Approach the world with **Love**
- Fight **The Courageous Fight**

Light *"Darkness cannot drive out darkness; only light can do that. Hate cannot drive out hate; only love can do that."*

One important thing to keep in mind is that those who oppose us feel just as strongly about their platform as the Tea Party supporters. Those who shout slurs of tea bagging, redneck, racists are doing so in darkness. Our response must be light. We cannot allow ourselves to taint our movement by succumbing to the will of darkness for that will only further divide the country and unhinge our message. The way to respond and to retaliate is in love and concern. We can correct our adversaries where they are wrong, but in doing so we must put on the armor of Christ and counter them in love and light. How do we do this? We don't attack back. We respond with the fundamentals of our message and apply the message to the issue only, not the person.

Our Neighbors *"We have flown the air like birds and swum the sea like fishes, but have yet to learn the simple act of walking the earth like brothers"*

At a class I taught this past year, "Lessons learned from the Civil Rights Movement," a question was raised of who the Tea Party should accept and reject. I thought the question related to rhetoric, but the class was thinking in terms of an individual's lifestyle. Specifically, a gentleman wanted to know the Tea Party's position on women who were pro-choice, or gay members in the Party. My short answer was that the Tea Party's message cannot be about rejection. We are called only to love our neighbors as ourselves and love God with all our heart. This is a message of acceptance. It isn't up to us to reject someone based on a lifestyle choice. It isn't our calling.

Immediately, a lady raised her hand and countered this saying, "I do think we should be careful about who we let into our movement. We don't want to weaken our message." It struck me for the first time that there must be many more believers with this point of view where she came from. God is love – surely and truly. Part of us being embraced in that love is to show actions of love. I don't believe God wants us here rejecting HIS children in order to defend Him or to keep a message purified.

None of us are worthy. Except by the grace of God do we even live and breathe to regret our sins. How can anyone go about rejecting another without knowing the character or the heart of the person simply based on the decision to abort a child, or that they are homosexual? In my more stubborn years, I looked down on these issues as well, thinking that I was more fit spiritually. Well, at least I… But if I say that, of course, I am loathe to look towards my own direction of sin. For the fact that I have not been faced with certain obstacles and decisions are for God's grace, not a testimony to my own strength and moral courage.

Perhaps the gay man has shown strength and moral courage in areas where I have been weak: patience and long sufferance. The woman who has had the abortion is a charitable and loving philanthropist with virtues of self control and a kind tongue whereas we are quick to scorn, easy to rile, and slow to give.

Jesus showed us the best example. King of kings, he came to earth in poverty and humility. He went straight to the weak and lowly: the tax collectors and the prostitutes. Are we too good to stand on principle with a gay man or woman, or a woman who has had an abortion or supports it? Most certainly we are not.

Love *"Love is the only force capable of transforming an enemy into friend."*

One particular goal we must strongly work on is to re-define what it means to be a conservative. For too long we have been shackled to ideas of narrow mindedness and stymied as bigoted hypocrites. We must make an effort to give a better PR campaign that expresses who we are by our hearts and our intentions for humankind.

I know we have our Christian beliefs of pro-life (I am too) and heterosexual marriage (I believe in that too), big BUT here, BUT it is only our obligation to keep our own house clean as we see fit. If we come across a neighbor whom we believe to keep a dirty house, is it Holy to keep them out of our own house saying that ours is too clean to receive them? Loving our neighbor as we love ourselves doesn't mean that we love the way they keep their house; it means we love them for being part of God's creation. We can love our neighbor without being fond of her and "approving" of her. We can love and want the best for any person without addressing the state of their house.

Besides are we keeping our own house clean merely to be above our neighbors, or to boast superiority in the face of other's shortfalls? Or are we keeping our house clean so that it is pleasing to God and to ourselves? If it is the second of the two, we should know be content and thankful that we have a gift of servitude in our hearts. If it is the first of the two, then we must surely acknowledge that while our house is clean, our hearts are not.

Whenever a Christian has an opportunity to show love to someone with whom they think they should not approve, it is a crucial moment to show the love of God. It is chance to be an example of his light and to hope for a positive change without demanding it. For we are not in a place to demand anything of anyone else. We can only hold ourselves accountable. What better way to bring out the best in someone else, than to first offer the best of ourselves.

Conservatives can no longer be the party of behavioral rejectionism wherein it does not directly affect our independent liberties. If we do not show love and inclusion then we condone hate. We give our enemies permission to hate us in return. If we want to change the cycle of hate, let us be the first to throw down the gauntlet of love, the only power strong enough to cast out hate.

The Courageous Fight *"If you will protest courageously, and yet with dignity and Christian love, when the history books are written in future generations, the historians will have to pause and say, "There lived a great people - a black people - who injected new meaning and dignity into the veins of civilization."*[4]

Oh, Lord, I pray. Let us leave a legacy of dignity and let it go viral, rippling and infecting all of civilization for generations to come. Let is set off beams of light and spark joy, love, and gratitude for humankind. For we are

God's divine creation put here for no nobler, yet no more challenging task, than to love one another.

The best and most beautiful thing Glenn Beck did to restore honor at his 828 rally was to tell people to, "leave your signs at home." I don't think all signs are bad, but when people show up with messages that are not cognizant to the issue, it drowns out what is really important. And what a mighty rally it was even without them. It was a vision of peace, unity, and understanding. Rather than dilute the occasion, gathering without the signs let all the light from above shine down on every soul who came to witness a restoring of honor.

The giftedness of Martin Luther King and his call for non-violence was that he called for dignity. We too must march to that same beat, letting dignity and grace be our redeeming force in our protest.

What we say is just as important as how it is said. We must march and protest, but we must do so in the sway of grace and poise. We can speak softly letting our votes be our stick.

What was a political movement and political philosophy now has the potential to be something much greater than all of this. The Tea Party movement has been called a restoration of many things: the Constitution, honor, greatness, liberty. I see it as all those things, but lately I see it as an opportunity to restore each other towards humanity and be part of a movement to deliver our nation back to God.

We need help to do this. Our power alone is not sufficient in this great endeavor to restore our country to humanity and honor. We require the strength and omniscience of a higher power. In all that we do, we must call on our Holy Spirit. We must diligently rely on a divine will and unassailable force of goodness and goodwill. We must invoke our own Trinity, in the name of the God our Father, the Son, and the Holy Spirit.

ADDENDUM

The Tea Party has grown up alot since 2011. They've produced stars like Ted Cruz, created a gain in the Republican House and Congress, fragmented the Republican Party, and have created so much noise within the base that the Republican Party barely has a discernible voice. There are so many candidates vying for the 2016 Presidential nomination that the Republican Party's identity crisis now seems like collective multiple personality disorder.

There are almost too many ways to be rightwing: Establishment Republican, Conservative Republican, Tea Party Republican, RHINO (Republican in Name Only) or Moderate, Libertarian (Rand Paul), Christian Conservative Republican. No one has any idea what it any of it means or what they stand for. The prevailing thought though is that most people can tell you what or who they are AGAINST: helping the poor, immigrants, Obama, freedom to choose, gay rights, women's equality and empowerment, economic opportunity for the underrepresented, black lives, taxes, abortion, and gun laws, the environment. It's a bad rap and one that is hard to beat. And, their base and those who see nothing wrong with this list is shrinking.

I ran for Governor of Texas for a few reasons. As a voter, I grew tired of being presented the same rotation of status quo candidates. I felt there was really no choice in statewide office in Texas. Candidates entered the ballot as if in procession, taking turns moving up the ladder until the baton was passed for their tenure. This couldn't be a healthy nor clean process that served voters, the underrepresented, and pushed humanity forward.

As a political pundit and talk radio show host, I was becoming uneasy with hearing and looking for the benefit of the doubt among these status quo candidates were saying about women, minorities, poverty, and our president--even though I disagreed with him at the time. I still believed in the principles and ethics of conservative values, but I longed to get behind a candidate I believed in, who expressed values of faith, hope and charity, and who wasn't part of the establishment. When it was clear, this type of candidate didn't exist, at an appointed time when all these issues were elevated, I stepped up to be the candidate I wanted to see and to deliver the message I wanted to hear.

Because of my speeches and television appearances, I was immediately defined as a "Tea Party Candidate." It was a label that I frankly wanted relief from and I sought to distance myself from its implications. It also became clear as I relied on God's voice to determine our agenda (something that drove me and my team nuts) that the message he sent me to deliver wasn't one that they would get. "We are in a spiritual battle for the hearts and minds of our people, not a political one. The only way we can win is to be a force of love not laws, economic principles, and politics."

Our agenda was poverty. Bringing economic and entrepreneurial opportunity to the nearly twenty-percent of working Texans living in poverty.

Representing the underrepresented. Change and challenge disability laws that kept parents from medicating their children with disabilities they way they saw fit, undoing the unfairness of limits to disability claims, reforming education so one's zip code didn't determine the quality of a child's education, and bringing dignity to working immigrants.

Life. We challenged the notion that being pro-life was about the law but that it was about women's rights and the empowerment that women need to honor their own lives and bodies. We wanted to redefine the life issue as about love, over legal ease and moral condemnation.

And, finally that to be a conservative was about more than being against Obama. It was to be for people.

I wanted desperately to share this message with all the Republican women's groups who had once welcomed me, but my presence now was that of an outsider, a traitor. They were afraid to host me. Intimidated by the power of the presumptive nominee. And so, at first, much of my message sat idle and untested.

It would be the Tea Party who would acknowledge and accept our campaign. The Tea Party groups invited me to forums, made a place for me on the stage, took signs to put in their yards. Here I was trying to distance myself from the only group who saw us as relevant. It is safe to say that if it weren't for the Tea Party, our campaign would have struggled even more than we did. We were climbing uphill all the way and not only was the Republican establishment not helping, they were throwing stones downhill to trip us up. Thank God the Tea Party offered us a little rope.

What's more, the message I delivered about dignity for immigrants, love in the life issue, and battling poverty didn't fall on deaf ears as I expected it would. I was timid to deliver messages about love and acceptance to a group known for their take no prisoners approach to the Second

Amendment. I was advised to simply stay with the "secure the border," script when it came to immigration, open carry on guns, and boo to Wendy Davis. But this was not the message I was called to deliver.

When I finally got up the courage to deliver my message with gusto and conviction, I found the Tea Party a rapt and very moved audience. When I told the parable of the workers in the bible in relation to immigrants, they were at first quiet and then reflective. Thier faith and reverence for the scriptures, God's living word stirred.

Say what you will about members of the Tea Party. I still stand behind the notion that they are largely misunderstood. With the right candidate and reminder of our call to serve Christ's agenda and not our own they could be awakened towards servant leadership that would bring healing, unity, and grace to this world.

Unfortunately, too many standing up for leadership play up on division and rhetoric. Rather than use the gospel to share the good news that because much is given much is expected and that a God who can surely feed thousands with five loaves of bread and two fish can multiply our abundant lands, resources, and opportunity to the poor, too many standing up to lead misuse the gospel to deliver bad news about the savagery of the left, the perils of the economy, the dangers of poor, unskilled and uneducated immigrants, and immorality of the lost in order to mobilize good people into tactics that look more like fear and hate than love and service.

Our patriotism cannot define our values, nor can it be the standard by which we accept and judge others. How I wish our campaign had more time to keep opening eyes and changing hearts about our true role as warriors for Christ.

That is not to preach, convert, and direct others in activism but to love so fervently that we open people's hearts making way for the power of God's love and mercy to accomplish what political muscle cannot. Can we set our patriotism and our right to "our rights" aside so that we can be part of a miracle, not a movement.

"First, pride in one's people is a good thing, but when the power and prosperity of the nation become unconditioned absolutes that veto all other concerns, then violence and injustice can be perpetrated without question. There is no precise way to define when patriotism has crossed over into racism, oppression, and imperialism. Yet no one denies that nations have slid down that slippery slope." Reinhold Niebuhr

SECTION III
GOD

FAITH

Real Love

"Real love, I'm searching for a real love, someone to set my heart free"
Mary J. Blige, "Real Love"

It would be silly of me to ignore the fact that you may be the reader who is not a Christian, or more to the point, an atheist, without a God or any higher power to which you ascribe and therefore relate to. I cannot attest with any degree of truth that you won't find this section to be a bunch of hooey. And I will not try to. Also, I will not – not because I do not wish it for you, but because this section isn't an attempt at miraculous Christian conversion.

I am not a minister or a preacher, just, a person who loves the Lord and struggles each day to live up to His love and His commandments. I am not claiming to be perfect, nor am I trying to minister to your perfection. The goal of this section is to make people realize the true and real love of God that is living inside of us. That we can realize fully who we are, and God's intentions for our greatness and goodwill in His glory, is my hope for our country. On a smaller scale, if we can just individually heed what our Kindergarten teachers told us, "do unto others as we would have them do onto us," this would be a tremendous feat as it is.

God is a given in this world, and in this country to be sure. To discuss Obama, the Tea Party, and the direction of this country without discussing God's presence and will for us would make no sense. God is and always has been the center of everything in America. Without addressing God, there is no point to exploring the how and why of Obama or the purpose of the Tea Party.

All things in our lives, good, or bad, are a mirror standing before us to reflect our connection and our relationship with God. Obama matters only because of God. The Tea Party is relevant so as to lead this country back towards God. They have started us on our way, now it is up to each of us to walk towards God' light and perfect love.

Chapter one of Rick Warren's *The Purpose Driven Life* is, "Without God, Life has no Meaning." The same could be said for America. America has no meaning without God. 'In God We Trust.' 'One nation under God.' 'America…God shed his grace on thee.' Our country has a long and deeply established relationship with God. Everywhere we turn, we are reminded of how our forefathers relied on the wisdom of our Heavenly Father to lead and set the tone for America. God is on our money, He is in our pledge, our patriotic songs, and more importantly he is in this nation's heart.

It is impossible to love America and respect her founding without accepting that this vast land of ours has always belonged to God. Her founders, immigrants, her soldiers, her lands keepers – the farmers and the slaves – have always prayed and looked to Him for their protection and the direction of their lives. As hard as one might try to disrupt this truth in keeping with the practice of religious freedom, God is a constant and beloved divinity that has been crucial America's formation and our greatness. He is even more critical today for our healing and human connectedness.

This is not to say that God has approved of us all of the time, nor have we always relied on His will in our political and daily life. We have fallen. We have not always known best. But never before have we been so lost as a nation. We've lost touch with who we are and who were created to be. If we are going to restore greatness and goodwill to this country, we have to start by recognizing God again as our Saviour. We have already begun rediscovering this country again. Now we will also need to rediscover ourselves in Christ. We can do it if we rely on God to help us just as we have done in the past.

We must first understand that we are HIS. Everything is His. He is the King of Kings. This land we love, HIS. Knowing that we are HIS was the sustenance immigrants fed on when their stomachs were grumbling. It is what led them to this land with nothing more than a few coins in their pockets and with their family tearfully waving in the distance. Knowing that we are HIS has been the freedom the slaves had in their souls when their bodies were not. He is what kept them singing HIS glory and songs of thanksgiving. Even though man's freedoms eluded them, God freed their souls with the promise of HIS love and eternal life. They sang. Prayed. They were faithful and found joy and goodness in life in spite of their circumstances in the world. Such is the peace that can be found in God, *"And the peace of God, which transcends all understanding, will guard your hearts and your minds in Christ Jesus."* Philippians 4:7.

Our hope has always been in God. Our faith is in his power and the destiny of his words. We are His. Where we have fallen short we fall down into the arms of forgiveness and love. Where we cannot find freedom in man or law, our soul rests in the freedom of righteousness that only his glory can provide. Where money can provide no peace and freedom in man no understanding, God's kingdom is a refuge for wisdom and discernment.

Falling in love with anything other than this is an infatuation. We never knew real love with Obama, or anyone else. Only Obama, we thought, was "the one." He told us what we wanted to hear. Here is the genius of God. We needed Obama to get us home. You might say he did show us towards real love. In his quest to make us a "more perfect" union, Obama has unwittingly led us towards perfection in the direction to God's perfect love. In turning ourselves over to him we are made perfect in his image. This love carries hope, change and true promise not in the passive nature of the world, but in the active discipline of our values, prayer, thoughtfulness, and love for one another spilling over.

CHAPTER EIGHT

Why Government Cannot be God

"Wherever politics tries to be redemptive, it is promising too much. Where it wishes to do the work of God, it becomes not divine, but demonic."

Pope Benedict XVI

Have you ever heard anyone say, "My Government has been so good to me?" If not by the grace of President X," we would be lost. Did anyone go tell it on the mountain, over the hills and everywhere that Barack Obama was born? Heaven and earth are not full of the glories of man.

Our American Government was designed to have very limiting powers for a reason. Our Government was founded based on the all men being created equal and these rights of equality coming from the creator, GOD. There is good reason our government should be run based on the consent of the governed.

Our founders had fled the evils of a Government ruled by the vices and aristocratic grip of man. They had usurped the people's humanity and God's law. As such, our founders knew that God's law and the consent of his creation was an imperative in American freedom. They put a constitution and a Declaration of Independence in place to guard against a tyrannical and self-imposing government that aimed to subvert God's will for his people: life, liberty, and the pursuit of happiness.

We are to live for God and no one else. We are to fear God, not man. Fearing God gives freedom. Fearing of our

Government as Thomas Jefferson wrote, tyranny. "When the government fears the people, there is liberty, when the people fear their government, there is tyranny."

The same can be said when the people look to their Government to do things that only God can and should be counted on to do. We have been led down a path of redemption through Government and man. This is all false. Our nation was never founded in hopes that our Government knew what was best for all men. In keeping with this the Government role is and should be limited to matters of self-defense, to protect the rights of the people that were endowed by their Creator, and to uphold the laws that were approved by the consent of the Government through the courts. Government is now trespassing into a territory for which they have not the authority, nor the bandwidth to understand.

To some degree I feel sympathy for Obama. We are the ones who allowed ourselves, even handed ourselves over to be seduced. The seduction became mutual as we fell so deeply into his spell, that he too was taken by his own potion. He has tried so hard therefore to live up to the messianic role we thrust him in.

Obama may be inadequate, but his deficiency isn't unique. No man could have fulfilled the grand delusions he offered or the lived up to our expectations. Consider this for a moment. We were asking for an America where every man, woman, and child is fed, clothed, educated, healthy, happy, content, wise, and kind all on the whimsy of hope and without any will or action of their own, yet, all on their own. We wished for an America that could conquer the ills of suffering, imbalance, inequality, and prejudice all on the words and symbolism of a mixed race President? We wanted all of this devoid of any spirituality or divine intervention.

It gets worse. We expected every American a guarantee of life and liberty without the expectation of their own pursuit. We were to obtain this without having to lift a finger ourselves or by at least getting on our knees in prayer. Doesn't this sound more than too good to be true? It sounds like a fool's dream. It has none of the excitement, joys, thrills, hope, expectation and trials that life is. In fact, it isn't *living* at all. It sounds exactly like life without God – meaningless and worthless to humankind. It is an evangelist Government where Government is not just trying to replace God, but seeking to be God.

What has happened to us this past decade with Obama and the Tea Party was a necessary progression towards God. It doesn't matter that the Government's intentions are ice cream dreams for all, or goodness. Their motivation and their self aggrandizing arrogance that *they* can make all our hopes and dreams come true is wrong. There is no fairy Godmother, no leprechaun granting three wishes.

But God doesn't profess to offer us a free ride to happiness and joy without ever a need or want in life. With God, life isn't a magic field of dreams and desires come true on hope alone. Instead, God offers us a life with Him. He calls for a love relationship. God offers us real love. This isn't a love full of false hopes and millionaire dreams. This real love is a promise of humanity where seeking and finding Him gives no limits to how high we can soar. As we strive to be better with His grace, the world for us is better too.

God's love call us to be worthy through His grace. On our own, we can do nothing. Politics can do none of the things that God can do. Nor can it set right the courses of our lives that have gone off track, or right the evil doings of the past. Every time it has tried to do this mending and repairing of natural order, it has failed.

If Government were able to be God, it could set a mandate that everyone be good. It would certainly have the power to do so, but since we have been ordained by God with free will, Government simply falls short of being able to do the things that only God can do. Where Government seeks to bring justice, equality, and offer peace it fails because Government is only a hierarchy of men not Gods; human beings who simply fail where they try to replace God.

We are unique; therefore, Government cannot make us equal; God has already done that.

I was recently awed watching Martha Stewart beguile me (from my couch) and a wide-eyed audience over one of her shiny gift baskets. In it was a jar of honey, "from my own bees," she gleamed. The audience continued to ooh and awe over her perfectly folded fitted sheet and her cucumber infused vodka and fresh squeezed yellow tomato juice for "the best" bloody Mary. (And to think we'd gotten by all these years using V-8). It was a display of perfection and gold ambiance that I would love to see over and over. But woe to the woman who will go on her merry way home and do her best Martha impersonation only to find that mimicking "perfection" isn't nearly as fun as watching it, or just being served it afterwards.

Fearfully and Wonderfully

Psalm 139:16 declares that we are "fearfully and wonderfully made." This is the best and most true reason I can think of that explains why the Government cannot be God no sooner than you and I can be Martha Stewart. We embrace the notion that we are different and unique in logical terms but, we have a harder time understanding just how distinctive we are spiritually in Christ. God knows our diversity through and through and it goes beyond the shape of our eyes, the contour of our mouth, or the color of our skin. In us are divine light, gifts, talents, dislikes, and many places for the Holy Spirit to dwell and make us one of a kind. Therefore only God can help us realize our greatest potential and greatest service to humankind.

That we are one of a kind prohibits the contrived concept of fairness and the ability of the Government to legislate equality. Our government cannot make us equal any more than they can have the sun rise. Our Father in Heaven does both. The Government didn't create us; therefore, they cannot equalize us any more than David Copperfield can make a man vanish into thin air. Like magic, this notion of Government equality is but an illusion.

You may be deceived into thinking the Government has reversed laws of inequality. Martin Luther King fought for the government to stamp out discrimination and make laws equal between black and white. Even so, Martin Luther King's call was not for Government to give equality, but for the Government to *recognize* what the founders wrote and what God makes true: that all men are CREATED equal. That creation doesn't come from Government. That creation comes from God. The Government was only acknowledging that it had no right to enforce "separate but equal" because equality was already granted from on high in our very existence.

We are all equal in God's eyes, but God's view of human equality is much different than the worldly view. In the world we rate equality in terms of opportunities and outcomes – fixed or otherwise. A noble idea, but one that hardly works in a spiritual sense. Might work great if we were a bunch of cells and wires, but we are colored by God's strong hands. A God, who colors with many more brilliant shades and hues than our eyes have ever seen.

Our very existence is unequal from birth depending on where we were born and to whom, from which country, city or state, down to our county and year of birth. Never mind our genetic heritage, we can no sooner be equal at birth in the worldly view than we can all grow up with the grace and legs of a Baryshnikov, the voice of Billie Holiday, or the hoop skills of Michael Jordan. Government can neither grant up the proper opportunity to these gifts, nor can they devise the desired outcome of their success. Presuming equality of opportunity and outcome at birth for every person could not be considered living, let alone living with purpose.

Why do we have little problem accepting that scientifically we extremely different? We are told that every fingerprint from person to person is completely genuine and unmatched by another. We accept this. Why then do we believe we can robotically level the playing field where each of us is uniquely designed internally?

Say I am the woeful woman who goes about trying to imitate Martha Stewart's perfect ideal. I decide to keep my own bees and make honey following Martha Stewart's instructions exactly. You be the taster. You might taste my jar and then Martha's and detect no similarities in either of them. Why not? I did exactly as Martha instructed with all things being equal; location, weather, processing. Still, you claim Martha's is fruitier and mine nuttier. Mine may be no worse, but it is not the same.

I may have an advantage in precision where she has an eye for details. She cannot resist improvisation (unknowingly to me), whereas I follow the recipe to the line. Then there is you, the taster with your subjective palate. You may have let her dainty foil wrapping sway you before you even tasted her honey. Whereas my drab gray cloth lost me points from the get go.

We are unique. What we offer and receive from the world is shaped by a myriad of experiences and microscopic details about us that no one else can divine. Here lies an inevitable bias that is life. This is the wonder of God. This is Life worth living. What we do with that life is largely up to us. This is our free will. The more we rely on God's direction in our lives, the more joy and peace we find. The more freedom, opportunity, and equality we have in spite of and independent of the world.

The Same in God's Eyes

So if we are all created so uniquely and without sameness to one another, how then are we equal and the same in God's eyes? We are equal in our humanity. Our sameness is in the value of our souls. God wants each of us and our souls equally: you, me, the beggar on the corner, the prostitute on the dark corner, the drug addict, the murderer, the preacher, and the saint. He wants a relationship with all of His children. He wants us and our kitchen sink thrown to Him so that he can be all to us. He wants us all equally to share in His Kingdom and to have a relationship with him. Each one of our hearts and souls is precious to Him and equal in value. We are priceless to God. We are connected in our humanity in this truth. This is the core of humanity.

Now do you see why Government falls pitifully short? Almost always in order to make society better from Government's perspective, the Government must assume that some group of persons are worse off, or are worse in character than another. Here they are overreaching into humanity and creation for which they have no role. And when they insist on doing so, they fall into the trappings of evil.

Governments have tried in the past to upend God's humanity. This has led to the Holocaust, tyranny, and slavery. In order for the Government to try and convince each one of us that they can make us equal, they must first remove us of our humanity, or seek to redefine it altogether. Once our humanity is stripped away, the Government's intentions invite evil among men. When men play God, they don't often play nice.

Humanity also gets diminished when Government portends to look out for "the little guy." How can the Government do this when they have no clue who the little guy is, what his passion is, what he was made to do? How can they look out for someone they cannot even see? Is the Government omniscient? Which President ever had authority over time and space? Besides this, the big guy needs love too. Does Uncle Sam just throw the big guys to the wolves? Who will look out for them? And, without knowing the ways of their heart and spirit, how does the Government judge who is "little" and who is "big" among us?

Because the Government sees none of us in spirit, they deal with us in number only: social security number; numbers on our paycheck; numbers to calculate how much in taxes we will pay; poll numbers based on where we live; poll numbers based on how we vote; demographic numbers telling them who to target for social programs; demographics numbers to show who lives in red or blue states. Numbers and percentages have nothing to do with humanity.

The best they can come up with is to take those who stand out in some low or high percentage compared to the whole sum and take from those in the high and give to the low. Another tactic is to feed those on the low end of the odds tall tales about how there day will come just as soon as those in the higher percentages are as low as them. This hardly makes for common sense or equality. Wouldn't those with your best interest want you to rise up higher and those up high even higher still? What kind of protector seeks lowliness among his people in the name of helping others?

What these numbers don't reveal are the history and the spiritual matters of yourself thrown in: your mother died when you were ten so you have always learned to take care of yourself and your siblings. You've worked since you were fourteen years old. As respite from the pain of your family's loss, you started baking cakes and pies to add some joy. With a little persistence, luck, and knack for precision in baking, you now own the largest cupcake franchise in the world. Some looking at you as a number, might say you are a big guy now.

To the Government you are a glitch in the system of equality and fairness. (What of Betsy round the corner after all who never learned to bake and is rubbing nickels together to make ends meet?) To God, you are a symbol of His glory. God has used your suffering for good. Your struggle has become a reward towards humanity. Where the Government will punish and tax you for this success and see you as a high number to be lowered, in God's eyes you are a spirit and a beam of light that He wants to catch fire and ignite the souls of your sisters and brothers. You are here to spread the good news! Tell everyone what He has done. Blessed is the One who comes in the name of the Lord. Heaven and Earth are full of His glory. Hosanna!! Hosanna! Hosanna in the Highest!!

Before we let out our first breath and take our first step, God formed us, thought about us, and knew He wanted us for His glory and His kingdom. We are fearfully and wonderfully made in his image to share in a love relationship with Him. He can do that. All that we hope to be? Well, He put in us the potential to become. All that we are not; He wants to help us become. He has us all figured out and he still wants every part of us. He wants to protect, love, and lead us to salvation from the world. And, in the world he wants us to be a reflection of his love and light.

Nothing in who we are: our skin color, hair texture, length of limbs, eye color, and penchant has been left to chance. It is all done for us to work towards our human good. Everything created in us, in collaboration with the Holy Spirit works to benefit us for HIS glory.

All that we are, He wants. He knows we are wretched, jealous, envious, poor, tired. He knows we are broken. He is God who makes all things new. Let Him take us and may we be a prize for His glory. Let God show off in us. Let Him cherish us and set our hearts on fire.

God is Love

But never, never pin your whole faith on any human being: not if he is the best and wisest in the whole world. There are lots of nice things you can do with sand: but do not try building a house on it. CS Lewis

We hedged so many hopes and dreams on Obama and the love we felt. We built a house out of sand. We now find this house of sand in utter collapse. Nothing built by hammer or hand. I've said before this wasn't all Obama's fault. We were not ourselves. We'd so removed ourselves from who we were that this made us fall for infatuation.

In the coming of Obama it was very interesting that so many labeled him as a messiah, both facetiously and metaphorically. We all knew that no one really believed he was the second coming of Christ, but there was something about Obama that produced an automatic halo.

He is chosen. He is gifted. He is appealing. Though what he wasn't was new. He was only new to us, because we'd allowed ourselves to slip into false ideas about greatness and see hope as a passive entity. We wanted him to be all, but we soon found out that were hoping for something in him that neither he nor any other man is capable of producing. Obama is not hope. Government has no power to change where we do not abide. Hope and change is about a love relationship with God.

Obama was never the answer. The Tea Party is not the answer, but is leading us to it. Government wants to be the answer and has failed, though not for lack of trying. Any man and his governing body fail to be a solution to mass problems not only, because we are unique, but also because they are not love. Our relationship with them is not based on real love. Only real love has the power to conquer all. The love of man is insufficient. God's love is the only love with the power to take away the sins of the world.

God's love is completely unconditional and unchanging. God's love is eternal and is the only love that can give us peace. God wants to be that for us. When we call on HIS power and HIS Holy love to help us, we realize that it was God's love that conquered slavery. It was God's love that called Martin Luther King and Civil Rights protesters to march and claim their rightful place as God's child. No governing body, no man instilled that will and force in them to march and demand their rights. God did that. No man or governing force told Martin Luther King to let peace be his way. God's love did this.

God is real love. If we want to really fall in love, we have to accept that Government and man cannot love us the way God does. The love of man, your sister, your husband, mentor, wife, teacher, and whatever love Government tries to offer is inadequate compared to the supreme love of God. They way He loves us and can fulfill us is unmatched by any person, possession, or purpose on earth. So deep and overflowing I don't think we can fully grasp the beauty and wonder of HIS love. We can't even love ourselves and our children half as much.

Government Doesn't Give Hope or Make Change

"Lord Have Mercy." "Thank God" "Thank Goodness" "Bless you" I could go on and on with expressions in which we praise and call on our Lord in good times, and in bad. Even in the simple act of sneezing, we say "God bless you." In our darkest hours, it isn't the mighty hand of Government or any man's we seek, but the grace and power of our Lord. So it is in the blessings of life.

When a child is born, does any person thank their Governor, President, or political party for the new miracle of life bestowed upon them. Living and bringing in new life is not the act of anything involving the world. Life is an intimacy of adding to God's kingdom. He legitimates life through creation. No life is an accident to God.

When a loved one is lost, have you ever heard anyone say, "Why, oh why, President Reagan?" We do not look to Government, our political party, or the world order to explain or give meaning to life or death. They aren't qualified to give us any meaningful answer. The Holy Spirit within us forces us to call out to God. In our strife, woe, worry; in our exuberance, God is with us. God is an undeniable presence in our lives, culture, and politics both metaphorically and realistically. Those who say or think they don't believe in HIM are still forced to behold His power and reach in the faithful who believe more in Him than any human soul on earth. For even though He is not seen, my faith tells me that He is more real than me writing this and more alive in you as you read this.

God is Love. God is living. God is present in you and in me. We have the power of the Holy Spirit running through our bodies. We have this on a whim and at our beck and call. We have a direct line to Christ without picking up the phone. And, His line is never busy. He never asks us to leave a message. We have our Father on hand night and day, 24/7. We knock and the door is answered. Can you say this about your Congressman, your Government?

We cannot have proper hopes and positive change without God's real love. God's hope requires action. It requires an active faith of things promised but unseen. This is the faith that Martin Luther King knew. "I might not get there with you, but my eyes have seen the promise land." God's vision showed him this. His faith in God paved the way for his actions of peaceful protest and sitting in jail for what God told him was right and true.

It is imperative that hope be placed in our faith for God's plans. Hope placed in the wrong interest and entity can lead to whimsical ideas and casual attitudes about our responsibility to life. Hope placed at the feet of false idols leads to despair. We can have no real hope where there is no faith. And without acting in faith, hope is lost. This maze always leads right back to God. For hope in Government means faith in man, or, a false idol. In this type of faith, we are passive and sidelined. This kind of hope requires a wait and see mindset, a mindset very common among mistreated blacks before the Civil Rights Movement. (I am always astounded when I read the lines from Martin Luther King that some blacks wanted to be patient and wait on time to turn things around.) It offers no true opportunities for faith to exist. This is not hope at all. This is not faith. It is a promise of death and of hope dead on arrival.

If we decide that we must change, we must surely firmly affix ourselves to God's will and wisdom. Not all change is good change. And when we set out to change, we must be careful about what we are changing into. Most of us assume that a change is for the better, but how can we be sure of a positive correction without knowing and obeying the will of God. Simple. If we are changing to fit a man's ideal of who we ought to be; our change is no good. If we are changing and bending ourselves closer to our relationship with God and praying for the Holy Spirit to come, our change is good.

If when our Government asks us to change, we must untie ourselves to God and God's word, this change is the work of evil. Where our Government requires our change to part ways with our founding principles of Government being led by the consent of the Government, this change is corrupt.

If it is our aim to get our country back on track, we need a new source of hope – rather an old source not put to good use recently. God has always been there for us, waiting on us to turn back, use His power, and make a space for a relationship with Him. When we are an image of His love and hope, He is glorified, not man. If we glorify man and put our hopes in him, we are impoverished in spirit and leave less room for God's riches to work in us.

In God as our hope, we find an active and living force within us rather than a passive idea of hope that leaves us waiting and wishing and pontificating on the outcome. With God's hope we set in motion a chain of events that require us to change our individual selves for the better and deliver this country back to God's hands. Back to love.

We Are HIS

Before we are black, white, Latino, American, Asian-American, or anything else, we are first and foremost children of God. If we do not accept this first, all other parts of our life are spent in pursuit of answers. We seek peace and understanding, but never find it. Acknowledging and proclaiming ourselves as children of God is the first awareness of our freedom.

When we fully know we are HIS, we realize that the reason Government cannot be God is because Government is created by men. As in love, the Government will always fall short of offering us our proper due in life. Government cannot give us what it doesn't have. As children of God we are already the inheritors of much more than Government or man can profess to give us. God wants more for us than we can even dream for ourselves.

One day my father and I were talking and worked our way into a very profound and philosophical point. This happens frequently. My father who is never short of funny quirky opinions of life and how to make optimism out of tragedy once asked me a simple question?

"What if one day you received a phone call from a lawyer who told him that he was an estate lawyer and he had recently found property and wealth beyond your imagination in your name. Somehow this money and property had been misplaced all this time, but after careful tracking and testing, they have now traced it back to your family, making you one of the richest people in the whole world. What would you do?"

Knowing this is purely hypothetical I still indulged my father in his game by telling him that truthfully I wouldn't know what to do. I would try and lessen the financial burden for some I know; perhaps set up a foundation for giving.

My father and I talked about how we like so many other people would go about walking world differently in these new shoes. Perhaps we would walk with our heads higher above our shoulders; the small things wouldn't get to us nearly as much. We would be comforted and feel less anxious about our futures. We would tuck our kids in at night warmly lit by the security that they would inherit plenty when we were gone.

"Well, you just got the call," my father said. "You are one of the richest families in the world. You are the inheritor of abundant lands and you're the rightful owner to riches beyond imagination. Your Father is the King of Kings." All of that and more is yours because you are a child of God.

God is our King. We belong to Him. We don't belong to a chamber of Senators and Cabinet officials. We are free in Him. We are rich in Him. We are cloaked in the protection of His grace and love. To know and have faith that we belong to Him is to reach the sky. Our faith in this simple truth has the power to lead all men to goodness and goodwill where hope in Government is just a fairy tale. If only we would truly believe this about ourselves and one another we would fly... Our lives and our whole world would open up in love, hope, and faith to the glory of Christ everlasting. What God has created in us, let no man could put asunder.

There isn't a thing the Government can do for us or give to us that Christ has not already offered us in abundance. Can we get past our "show me the money" existence and our meek notions about God as our Savior long enough to reap the rewards of our chosenness and His love. It is time we proclaim boldly and without hesitation that He is worthy of our glory and praise. Let's shout with gladness that our Father is King of Kings and we want for nothing because we are His. Let God reclaim his rightful place in our daily lives. Or will we continue on lifting up man as a savior and wishing on stars that their false promises and hopes will create a true and positive change? We have to decide and we have to be ready. The true urgency of now is to put on the armor of God.

We will have to put on the armor of Christ. Because as we have seen, when we accept and believe in God's rightful place as King, we will be vilified, crucified, and ridiculed. Are you ready for the onslaught of insults? Are you ready for the silent betrayals? Are we willing to die for this love as Christ died for our sins? For even if we do not die for our cause such as Martin Luther King, this faith and acceptance requires us to die of ourselves – our wants, our desires, and our worldly hopes and accept the cup the Christ has given us and drink it to the bottom. This faith requires action, not just a lucky couch from whence we sit and root for one guy in the election over the other. This is real skin in the game. This is living God's word and following him in His love and His light. The only remaining question is how high are you willing to let God take you?

CHAPTER NINE

God's Law and the Conservative Character

"For as the body without the spirit is dead, so faith without works is dead also"
James 2:26

Once folks sort-a-kind-a know me, I receive queries and remarks on a regular basis about what it is like to be black, black, tall and athletic, black growing up in East Texas, driving while black, and being black and married to a Caucasian. Still being black and conservative in combination with all those things mentioned above gets most votes for eliciting intrigue.

The questions hardly offend. If anything I am flattered that somebody cares to know. Though some flatter and others bewilder. For example, a friend passed along a queer observation of my life and conservative values: What a surprise that my husband and I are an interracial couple. I didn't get it still. Well, the point is she continued, "One would think that conservatives would be opposed to marriage out of the racial boundaries. That is a more liberal thing to do. How can you be a conservative and married to a white guy and vice versa?"

News alert for liberals: Conservatives aren't the angry stiffs we are purported to be. We plant trees, drive Priuses, eat vegan (I try to at least once a week), serve meals to the homeless, and cry when dogs are run over. We are in your book club, your AA classes, and your farmer's market. We have even invaded your Hatha yoga class, NAMASTE.

Just as liberals some of us harbor prejudices, cut you off in traffic, eat too much, and owe lots of apologies that we are unaware. And all kidding aside, just as liberals claim, we also yearn for peace on earth, goodness and goodwill to all men, to feed the hungry, and clothe the poor, and to help the starving and ravaged children of Africa.

I understand how conservative values have become mixed up with passing judgment, bigotry, racism, and self-righteousness. The reason why is because we've left God out of the picture in explaining conservative values. I think George Bush was off to a good start with the compassionate conservative, but it really is about the Christian conservative; the daily conservative; the sinning and repenting conservative; the human and loving conservative.

Conservatives have a duty to redefine these values for ourselves and our country. The opportunity has come to remind this country and each other why we are conservative in the first place. I understand the hesitation. As a black conservative, the implication of a conservative mind and spirit implies social treason, betrayal, and brainwashing. I've also been accused of being mildly retarded by some who cannot understand what reason there is to be a conservative.

Conservative values are not about race and politics regardless of what liberals say. Conservative values for me are about putting our faith and trust in God into action in our daily lives. Conservative values are our faith in God's word and His will put into action. Faith without works is dead. As faithful children of God, we cannot sit idly by and say we love the Lord and withhold our obedience. Obeying him doesn't mean that we don't fail; it means that we keep trying and praying to the Lord that He strengthens us to keep obeying. Conservative values that align with God's word are about the fear of God.

The Fear of God

The fear of God gives many Christians and non believers trouble. Does this mean that God is a daunting and untouchable God who makes rules and ask commandments of us we cannot master? Are we burdened with extremely high standards as He holds a glorious heaven and His mansion of many rooms over our heads only to know we will not make it there? And, when we fail, we go to Hell?

Fear of God is neither of those things. Everything that is good is God. We should know this first and foremost. God isn't out there tempting us with sin in the first place. So if he is not tempting us, fear cannot mean to be afraid. We are not afraid of what is good, only of what is bad. Recognizing that sin, temptation, wicked thoughts, and negative emotions do not come from God is the first step to understanding the fear of God.

The second step is to understand that a relationship with God has nothing to do with success or failure. These, like fear, are worldly terms. A relationship with God simply means a daily reliance on His will and a surrendering of the worldly self. A relationship with Him is getting to know him and letting him work inside of you. The fear of God is therefore twofold: reverence and awe. God doesn't need us to obey Him out of fright. He wants our obedience out of love and awe of what following his ways can do for us.

Parenting is a good example. No parent puts boundaries and rules in place to harm their child. Likewise mothers and fathers don't go around demanding a child do his best in school and then offer them the chance to stay up until midnight playing Xbox. Whereby if the child chooses to sleep, they get a reward; if they choose to play the video game all night, they are grounded. The two are inconsistent. The parent simply wants the child to go to bed early, because he knows his son is likely to get a better result in school than if he stays up. The reward for both the parent and child is excelling in school. The rules are acts of love and a preservation of life.

I recall tearfully getting a spanking by my grandfather who would rather have his finger cut off, than to lay a hand on me. But I'd told a really bad lie and when he called my mother, she told him he had no choice. So he set out to spank me, but before he did he said, "This hurts me a lot more than it hurts you." I could see that it did. Punishing me was not something he wanted to do. He would have rather I not lie in the first place. He could have let me off easy, but to what end? For me to grow to be a pathological liar? My family wanted better for me. This is love. And forcing me to have a painful consequence is part of that love. For which of course, I am grateful.

There is no real love without rules and discipline. Can we have freedom without self control? Which child has the hardest time in adult life? Is it the one whose parent kept the closest eye out, or the one whose parent had no curfew, no boundaries along the way? The parent with no codes of conduct or boundaries for their child, may also say, well I still loved my child. How did they show it? Freedom without proper guidance and direction doubles as apathy.

The second part of the fear of God is to be in awe of His wondrous ways. Fear means a reverence that nothing is above Him and nothing is equal to Him. God is all and He is worthy of our admiration. A song that always reminds me of this is the U2's "Beautiful Day." I get chills thinking how God created the genius expressed through Bono and the lyrics of this song. You can feel God's hand in this music, "And see the bird with a leaf in her mouth. After the flood all the colors came out." Listening to this is to revel in the magnificence of God's creation and His gifts to humankind.

147

Taking note of all the beauty surrounding us: the stars, moon, the ocean, and the birds in the trees; this is the fear and wonder of God. When we follow his commandments and rules for our lives, we then come to see who we are part of this fear. We are fearfully and wonderfully made. Then shouldn't we be in awe of one another, giving all the praise and glory to Christ. This is the Fear of God.

Faith & Fear in Action

Who needs morality when we have technology, good intentions, and prosperity to keep us all happy? In putting God aside for so long in this country, we've gotten away from the fear of God and our conservative commandments. We've allowed the other side to distort these values and flip them upside down. We'd skated by for such a long time on diluted values, that the left almost had us fooled. We started believing that we didn't need conservative values and God's law in our lives.

This is a liberal lie. Happiness and peace does not exist outside of God. Freedom does not exist without discipline and diligence to our purpose. We are not good on our own; we require God's grace and support. We are not free simply because we can eat where we want and wear what we choose. Freedom does not mean a life without turmoil and conflict. We aren't here to be pacified and entertained each waking moment of our lives – this is your brain on drugs.

Freedom and peace comes from following the conservative path of God's laws. Notice I didn't say Republican or Tea Party, but conservative. There is a vast difference. Any person can be a conservative, not by their political party alone, but in living their daily lives. Conservative values are our faith in action and our commitment to God. Following a conservative lifestyle puts our faith into action and sets goodness and goodwill in motion. Life without morality and God's divine laws is spiritual slavery; a cage for the soul. No human being and no country can survive without firm moral laws forever. Civility requires a common humanity that is linked to a divine morality. This is the essence of humanity.

Conservative values are not about superiority of one person over another. They aren't meant as a way to dictate how one should live for the purposes of restriction, but freedom. Unfortunately, there are no short-cuts to morality. No fad diets or overnight sensations to strong character, courage, and freedom.

LIBERAL LIES & CONSERVATIVE TRUTHS

I commented that liberalism is diabolical and evil. I am not saying that Democrats are evil, or that every liberal person is evil; however, I am saying that the premise of liberalism leads to condoning evildoing and can work against common good.

When one examines exactly the main components of liberalism through behavior (i.e. abortion), ideology (superior beings and inferior beings), and purpose (freedom without discipline) the consequences can be nothing less than depression and devastation of a people who live and follow its philosophy.

I am not a conservative because of myself, or because I see other conservatives as such or having all the answers. I am a conservative because this view of life more closely resembles the commandments set by God, he who is all knowing and gives life. In fact, many successful liberals espouse liberal views for society, but when you look closely at their own path, they have in fact relied on conservative principles (a lot of it common sense) to get them ahead in life. Conservatives have allowed liberal lies to demure us into submission for too long. Conservatives have been afraid of their own strength. We know that conservative values are what made room for the liberal mindset to even exist. The conservative ways of this country led us to greatness and got us to the point where we can indulge in moral folly. In other words, when one is poor, even the worst of what is edible gets eaten. When there is plenty to eat, even good food goes to waste. Now that liberal ideology has us prowling for scraps, we find ourselves going back to what has worked before *and* where our souls tell us we belong: with God and his conservative laws for living.

No matter how appealing or how convenient for us, lies are extremely destructive. While the truth is often more difficult to accept and requires more of us, it does indeed set us free. Without speaking the truth and living it, we will not be able to break the cycle of evil and destruction that has been headed our way. We can no longer subsist on liberal falsehoods. Let's tell the truth about God and what true conservative values mean to the character and daily lives of the individual. The truth is goodness. The truth's opposite is a lie, evil.

Liberal falsehoods pave the way for the Government to try and act as God. They also make it easier to believe circumstances of poverty, discrimination, and injustices are beyond our individual control. Liberals would have us believe that without high-handed Government intervention, certain people would forever go disenfranchised and unaccounted. This simply isn't true. Accepting this to be true eliminates the need for God and a moral civilization. This opens the door for evil.

Instead of depending on good intentions, as many liberals often do, we can instead live according to God's commandments and God's laws. Living in His word can eradicate many of the problems we face in our society. God has provided us with a code for living that helps to shield us from poverty, racism, and inequality. Following the code individually helps us collectively.

Of course liberal logic puts up obstacles to these truths. They seek to undermine conservative values by saying that such values are bigoted and unrealistic. Liberals want us to believe there is no redeeming or emphatic moral code. There is indeed. And it is the conservative way of life that follows God's word.

Conservative Values are Based on Faith in God's Word

It gets no plainer than when Jesus says in John 14:6, "I am the truth, and the way, and the life." God, our Father, Creator of all things has left us with a guide to living, happiness, and peace. He also given us free will to follow or reject this guide according to our own wishes.

The Government certainly doesn't love us enough to let our free will reign. They want to legislate, tax, and regulate us into submission so that they can then determine who we will be and how we will live. This is not faith, hope, or love. It is slavery. It isn't freedom. Their idea of freedom is that in order to free everyone, some of us will have to be tied up first. There is no peace without knowing God's will and word for our lives.

God's Love
"If ye love me, **keep my commandments."** John 14:15

I was just about to leave for a retreat to center myself. I was struggling internally and questioning which way to go. Out of the blue, my aunt FeLisha visited. Sensing my inner turmoil she talked to me about my spiritual life. I really didn't want to hear it at the time; I wanted to shoot the breeze, or be left alone to consider which direction I would apply myself. Felicia persisted and what could I do? I was cornered. Besides, there was chip and dip and wine a plenty, and my auntie whom I never get to see. So, I listened.

"How are you with God, because me and God are like this," – as she made an "x" with her fore and middle fingers. A bit defensively, I told her about my bible study group (that I had just joined a month ago) and well, that I love God. This didn't do it. As my aunt pressed on, she finally came to tell me what I needed to hear. She said that my relationship with God was one-sided. Yes, I was praying and asking for things and counting on His grace and mercy, but I was inactive in the relationship. She said that God wanted me to get to know HIM. How? Through His words.

I went on my retreat with a completely different outlook on my relationship with God. All these years, I'd leaned on Him and counted on His guidance without really listening and understanding HIM. My faith was dormant and incomplete.

I began by familiarizing myself with The Ten Commandments, our moral laws from the Old Testament. These are the laws that God asks us to achieve for our own benefit. Though we fall short, we are loved and forgiven. The New Testament is our covenant with Christ that we are born again in faith. And "he whoever believes shall have everlasting life." Combined they are a model for living and living to our own individual and social good.

The first edition of this book included a list of the commandments that seemed to me very puffy and pretentious. It came across as preachy, legalistic and self-absorbed. Max Lucado makes a great point when he says that legalists trust in Christ a lot, but they don't trust in Christ alone." Reflecting on this point, Jesus says the greatest commandment of all is to love God with our whole heart and mind and to love one another as we love ourselves.

Conservative Values Don't Change

"Times are a changin'" don't apply to conservative values. Conservative values are intergenerational. What was good for our ancestors and our parents is good for us. Still, we try and bend the rules to ease up on the pressure. We don't want to work that hard, suffer that much, break our children's spirit. Our liberal way of life has tricked us into thinking that we are different. We no longer need to follow strict moral codes and listen to good old fashioned common sense. It simply isn't true. Loose living has never impressed anyone over time. "Times change, but people don't change," my mom always said. What was good and true for the human spirit in 1776 is good and true today in 2011.

When I had my first child, Bowie, I had high ideas how I would never spank; I wouldn't yell. Unlike how I was raised, I would let him explore and be himself. I wanted him to be able to make good choices. To me, this meant giving him an abundance of choices and helping him grow. I didn't want to parent and have obedience out of fear. I wanted him to obey out of love, learning and respect. I decided that my upbringing was too rigid for my children.

The bible says, "Teach a child the way he should go." It didn't take long for me to realize that a child's mind is not capable of making adult choices. More often than not I was put into the childish position of yelling more frequently than called for. We suffered the absurdity of a two-year-old setting the rules where full grown adults where following the directives of a person who had been in the world a mere 24 months!

One day I was having company and decided to clean my seat cushions. I stuck my hand between the folds only to bring back gobs of prickly crumbs, gooey globs of God knows what, and everything else in between. In keeping with my new age idea on parenting, I rejected my mother's restriction that kids only eat at the kitchen table as inhibiting and too strong. My kids were allowed to eat in the living room and watch cartoons. It took me a full hour to clean that chair and check the others. It took a month of redirecting and laying down the law for Bowie to accept always eating at the kitchen table. This is the way it should have been all along.

There is a reason for the restriction of conservative values. They teach us important lessons. Because times change, but people do not, conservative values are always true. It is always right to enforce boundaries, create smart habits, and redirect a child headed in the wrong direction. The direction could be running in the street, the arrogance of calling an elder by a first name, or the willfulness of talking back in order to get their own way. And yes, a little rat-a-tat-tat on the bottom for the willful "NO" or refusal to obey a command. All of these things instill values: self control, respect for others, and honoring elders.

Even the little values that seem insignificant and not to make a dent in our character, make a difference. Delayed gratification, learning that sex before marriage was wrong, calling adults Mr., Sir, and Mrs., and Ma'am was good for us then and will be good for our children tomorrow. Weakening the values doesn't make character stronger, it lessens us all.

Conservative Values Require More of Us
God's love is a love that says, "Whoever does not work shouldn't eat." (2 Thessalonians 3:10). This sounds cruel to some, but when we look at the power it holds for the individual, we know it means where we are capable, we should produce.

Something about "free" health care doesn't sit right even with those who cannot afford it. When we hear the statistic that 42 million Americans (1 in 8) are on food stamps – we know there has to be a better America out there. What have we done to diminish our greatness over the past forty or so years? And how can we find our way back to the land of opportunity?

It may sound just that the more fortunate should be forced to help the less fortunate. That is until we remember who we are. We are children of God. We are equal. I don't mean there isn't room for charity or that every single person can pull themselves up by their bootstraps, but I do mean that every person can and needs to be useful. Not rich, not beautiful, not lucky, not great in wealth and social stature, but useful. If we look at the conservative ideal that each of us has a purpose, a gift, and a talent, how could we accept that others among us not be required to offer their best effort?

Do we really mean to tell someone they are not useful without riches equal to their neighbor or the top one or ten percent of their neighbor? That there are those among us pre-destined for success, while some have NO chance in the world at greatness? What is this based on? Whose laws? Whose assessments? Man? They have no right to prophesize opportunity and destiny this way.

When one man tells another human being (who is mentally and physically able with strong breath in his body) that it is good and right for him to eat without hunting, working, cooking, or even having to fix their own plate, this isn't compassion and humanity. This is a superiority complex of the haves over the have-nots. The have-not has no reason to try and be the source of his own survival. With every free bite his humanity and dignity decays a little bit more until he can no longer feel worthy of his life. This is the work of evil.

It is lie that philanthropy is a one-sided salvation of giving and donating of resources and money. True giving is also about inspiring the receiver to knowledge and wisdom. The real goal is to not just have those in need get buy, but to edify their human spirit. Philanthropy of the spirit is to make the spirit realize it is worthy and capable of much more than they can receive in charity.

As Christians, we are called to make our brothers and sisters realize their own chosenness in Christ. Rather than thinking "it's better to spread the wealth around," as President Obama believes, it is of greater use to the less fortunate to not spread the wealth around, but to spread around the knowledge and formula for success in creating the wealth. Generating wealth should be the goal, not merely re-distributing it. Eventually the redistribution model will thin out as more and more of us decide to be takers instead of givers. Better to have more givers than takers wouldn't you say?

Of course, this isn't the easiest route to success. It requires a great deal more effort from the giver and receiver. Yet without this crucial element of giving, we've done nothing more than procure nice dreams for ourselves about our own generosity, or, played into the less fortunate's feelings of oppression and despair. Simply covering them with blankets of condescension and indignant justification to their situation is to ignore the purpose of their lives and the fight of their spirit.

By all means we are to give our first fruits, err on the side of generosity, and be charitable to those in need. I have yet to meet a person not willing to give. Usually we find that people are too proud to ask for help. At least it used to be. Part of our American spirit has been broken by excuses. We've allowed racism, bad childhoods, sexism, obesity, an unlevel playing field and other cons of the day as a reason to go easy on ourselves. At the first reckoning of failure we retreat and surrender in the comfort of these excuses. Where have we stowed away "if at first you don't succeed, "what doesn't kill me, makes me stronger," and "I can do all things in Christ who strengthens me?" Where has our true hope gone?

It is the responsibility of those who have been blessed and fortunate to get back to teaching men how to fish. And when we have them in the boat, we have an obligation to make them see their own way to victory and promise. We don't even have to preach to do it; we only have to show them the love of God by making them see that they are somebody. Anything less than this is not charity or hope, but arrogance and self-righteousness on the part of the fortunate.

Conservative Values are not political

We all love a label. We want to call a spade a spade. When someone can define themselves through a label of any kind it's a shortcut to getting to know what they believe and how they feel about certain issues. Political labels can be especially deceiving.

For instance, most blacks consider themselves Democrats. Democrats vote with the liberal agenda most of the time. Blacks have by and large been raised with conservative values, which should make them politically Republican.

A good case in point was in California during the gay marriage proposition. Democrats who can almost always count on the black vote, felt betrayed when more than eighty-percent of black Democrats voted against the proposition to support gay marriage, a conservative stance.

How we live is independent from how we vote. (I'll leave it for another book to pontificate on this), but, suffice it to say, conservative values have led to success and given us the freedom to be liberal. It's only through generations of conservative values, that we have the luxury to pontificate on how to spend other people's money on those who are unemployed or on Government assistance. Conservative values made this notion possible.

Conservative Values are the Antidote to Racism and Poverty

Like many other problem in our society that ail us, racism and poverty can be managed through conservative choices. What we have yet to accept is that some people would rather hang on to racism and poverty rather than commit to the actions they themselves must perform to change them. Who would want to be a victim of poverty if they can help it? Who would not want to end racism if they could help it? Plenty of folks, if it means they have to give up their Friday night out with the boys and pick up a second job bagging groceries to make ends meet.

Racism & Poverty

The statistic that 50% of American children and 70% of black children are born out of wedlock can be changed. Likewise, it should make us sick to our stomachs. Premarital sex is a matter of self control, not a matter of spontaneous conception. Do we teach children to honor this value of chastity out of love for themselves and their God? Or do we continue on the path of self indulgence where we are taught to indulge every carnal desire. Where pleasure and titillation by all means and at any cost can be rectified through a Government with crumbs to hand out?

Not treating sex as an action of love, reverence, and self control leads to personal and societal malice. Just look at the harm that it causes to poor children born to children. When their opportunities are diminished, and they are left to fend for themselves in life, racism and poverty get the blame, whereas lessons on love and self-discipline are never linked in.

Ending racism and poverty is a tough job. Today, however, it is also largely an individual and personal choice that takes thoughtful consideration of one's choices and actions. The opportunity for racism will persist as long as we deny people the power of their choice and hold them accountable to their actions. This is the same with poverty. How many success stories do Americans own of those who have made something out of nothing, and who have triumphed over adversity and poverty? They did so not by the withholding of gifts, talents, and money of another, but by turning their ingenuity and gifts into purpose.

How do conservative values serve as the antidote to racism and poverty? First, family. A child is more likely to have opportunity where she has two parents instead of one. Yes, it can be done with one, though why would anyone set themselves up to make it harder? "Honor your Father and your Mother." God knows we are to have each parent with us. He is ultimately our heavenly father, but so many children out of wedlock violate God's moral code.

A quick word about abstinence and young people. We hear so often that abstinence is so unrealistic. Kids will do it anyway. How can we stop sex? No one ever died from not having sex. Sex is about love and commitment. Taking time to discuss this with each other openly rather than simply saying sex is wrong or shouldn't be done is a part of abstinence teaching. Teaching the conservative idea of love and the spiritual connection between a man and a woman that sex is meant to be should be part of the curriculum as well. Discussing the harmful consequences of sex too soon beyond STD's and pregnancy might have more influence. Poverty, lower qualities of life, fewer choices, and diminished self-esteem are the traps we fall into when we trade in our values for a few minutes of pleasure.

"A Mind is a Terrible Thing to Waste" was the tagline for the United Negro College Fund I heard often growing up. When did we stop talking about the mind in our country, the soul, the spirit? We talk so much of the physical and the end result of poverty and racism, never acknowledging how we get there and how to retrace our steps to go in a different direction.

Conservative values are the new hope for change. Self- control and delayed gratification are the new stimulus. Something for nothing and chasing every new thrill is not part of the fabric of our society. It doesn't blend. It itches and is uncomfortable for a reason. It doesn't fit. It doesn't make sense because the Holy Spirit dwells within and calls us to a higher way to be.

The conservative value of thrift ties in with self control and coveting. Our pride in wanting to have the best and be seen as the best fools us into thinking we can shop and buy our way into greatness and importance. We will never be more important than God, nor should we keep the lie going that we must all try to be.

Seeking God helps us find a comfort in having enough. When we realize that enough is not having as much as your friend has, or driving as good a car as your neighbor, or having a home as big enough to be on MTV Cribs, we can create a space for poverty to leave us, spiritually and financially. Looking to God helps us see that we have idolized fortune and coveted things of the world. Knowing God is to have everything! Following his law and observing conservative values builds a character towards victory and greatness that money cannot match.

Conservative Values Link us to Humanity

The greatest lie we are living now is that there is no divine moral order, that there is no proper moral code in which to live. Though it may not suit our lifestyle choices and bend to our desire to sin, it does exist. Still, it isn't up to us to fix people. Only God can do that. It is only our human responsibility to acknowledge right from wrong and not make any concessions about it.

Right and wrong is not about choice. Right and wrong just is. Disagreeing with what is right doesn't make it wrong no more than calling a duck a pig makes it a pig instead of a duck. It's confounding that liberals who are adamantly against the euthanizing of pets, pet abuse, killing of any animal, can boil down the killing of a fetus as the right to choose. This is wrong. This doesn't fit into the circle of humanity. This is taking of life. We've wrongly inserted ourselves as the creator and have decided that we can give and take life. This is wrong.

Why is it wrong for a human being to kill a dog for no reason? Why was it wrong for Michael Vick to abuse and race those dogs? Because he is a human being and he should be held to a strict moral code. The same applies to why we should not take the innocent life of an unborn child. We know better. How we know better is tied directly to God's divine moral authority and his living inside of us. We know instinctively when we are wrong because God is living in us. God living in us is the Holy Spirit. In the Holy Spirit is our humanity and therefore our tie to morality. Or simply, right from wrong.

Man did not conjure up right from wrong. It is inherent within us. We know this because right and wrong are universal. Goodness and evil have the same characteristics all over the world. Stealing is wrong no matter where you go. Kindness is good and appreciated. A smile means the same in Timbuktu as it does in Gilmer, Texas.

Living these values is the active part of our faith and hope. The fear of God is the beginning of wisdom. This fear is what makes us wonderful. The fear makes us human.

THE CONSERVATIVE CHARACTER

Abiding by these commandments and following principles of faith, love, understanding, self control, and generosity amounts to the content of our character. Nothing in these commandments are made to harm us and nothing in the world can conquer them when we rely on God's strength in living them. A better question to ask is, can following these conservative values and submitting to the word of God, harm one's character, or worsen or cause destruction in a society? Of course it does not. Bringing them back and working diligently in our personal characters to follow them is our faith in action. Our faith in action is hope.

A conservative character places a "firm reliance on the divine." In this reliance we commit to freedom through discipline and obedience of morality and all that is good and right. We do our best to turn away from sin. And, above all if we do nothing else we can break it down to these two things: love our neighbor as we love ourselves and love the Lord God with our whole hearts. In Jesus name. Amen.

CHAPTER TEN

Yes, HE Can!

'Take up your cross and follow me'

Matthew 16:24

"Be still and know that I am God" is God telling us to trust in Him. The sorrow we felt for the past sins of slavery is that we thought Obama could correct what only God can heal. The inequity we sought to fix among men. God can level it out. The anxiety we feel over losing our homes and maxing out our credit cards. God can calm it. The desire to succumb to temptations of envy, jealousy, and revenge; God can stamp it out. The anger we feel at our neighbor; the fears we have about our children's education; the doubt that we are good enough; our concerns that our company will not have a job for us; the anguish over obesity rising while more and more labels tell us what to eat; the exhaustion of working three jobs, but still coming up short at the end of the month. GOD CAN CONQUER IT. Yes, HE can!!!

We fell for Obama because he represented a quick fix to so many problems we thought were too big for us. We see now, that we are the ones who must dig in to solve these complex issues and we need God's strength to get us through. Of course we can, but to whom shall we go? Luckily, we've found our way home. Are we ready to take up our cross and follow God?
God is ready.

God has been patiently waiting for us. And how good it is to be home or on our way there. We have missed God.

Coming home has not been easy. We took the long way home and suffered scrapes and bruises along the way. Where we were brought to our knees in strife, we are now on our knees, to pray.

If the Old Testament was our moral law from our Father, the New Testament is our Father welcoming us home with arms outstretched wide. God is happy to have us come home to Him; He sent his son Jesus to spread the good news and save us. In return we are also here to spread the good news and live in love and peace. Yes, the morality is still part of us, but we have been given redemption and salvation from our God.

Instead of making life so hard, we can simplify it to two things based on what Jesus commands of us: love our neighbor as we love ourselves and love the Lord with our whole heart. If we follow these two pearls of life, we leave peril behind.

Where we were broken, complacent, and searching for peace, God is a refuge. To take comfort in him and completely surrender to His will, we must acknowledge some of the traps we fell into from the beginning. We've been urged to contain our passion about God and to carry meek ideas about His role for us individually and as a nation. We must get rid of these false premises that have us caught in a cycle of dependency and spiritual oppression in order to thrive in His will. Three main false premises stand out.

False Premise 1: We Must be Tolerant

If tolerance means we have to tuck God away from our daily lives and that we cannot speak of His goodness and praise his Holy name, then forget it. It is too great a price to pay. It is necessary for us to lift God up in praise and call out His righteousness. We do this not only because He is worthy, but also because making these joyful noises, puts the joy into our hearts and connects us with the Holy

Spirit. We are a moral and religious country. There are many ways to navigate tolerance without letting go of God.

For a while straying from God didn't seem to have an impact on our lives. We were secure in our belief that we had our lives under control. For a while the white noise of our easy credit interfered with our connection to the Holy Spirit. And, this was part of putting tolerance and political correctness ahead of all things while keeping our affection for God at bay. We were told God belonged in the back of our lives as a matter of church and state. As a matter of religion, we should hold off on keeping with God until Sunday. And, though we strayed from home, God was with us. He was ready.

Since my mother is in education, we talk a great deal about education and politics. One day I remarked to her how I thought it was so awful that God was being removed from our lives in so many significant ways, namely, prayer in school. Mom quickly retorted that no one can prohibit prayer. No one can stop anyone from praying, anytime, anyplace. "God is everywhere. No one can stop a child from praying. You can show deference to God and bow your head and pray at school all day long if you want." Well, this is true, but still I felt God had been slighted. Before I could explain as much my mother as usual was several paces ahead of me and said, "God doesn't need your showy display of praying attention. He is a jealous God, not a pretentious one. He knows your heart and when you are praying. That someone sees you and approves of you or not, doesn't matter."

I was on the radio when a story broke in Georgia of a high school that began football games with the football team breaking through banners painted with bible verses. One such banner read Proverbs 16:3, "Commit to the Lord whatever you do, and your plans will succeed." The high school in Georgia had been creating these banners for years until they received notice that they were in federal violation of the first amendment. With regret, the superintendent was forced to have them pull the banners or put them in a discreet place on the football field.

Rather than retreat to an unseen place with their banner, these young Christians and their communities removed the signs but exalted God even higher by making individual signs for the game, wearing scripture painted on their bodies, T-shirts, and standing up for Christ. Whereas the banner was broken immediately after the team ran through, these signs and T-shirts were visible for all to see during the entire game. When asked about the effects of the having to remove the banners, one student replied, "You can take away our signs, but you aren't going to take away our beliefs."

> Onward, Christian soldiers, marching as to war,
> with the cross of Jesus going on before.
> Christ, the royal Master, leads against the foe;
> forward into battle see his banners go!

Tolerance doesn't mean that we silence our beliefs and turn away from God's presence in our lives. The bible tells us to pray without ceasing and to make a joyful noise. No federal law can contain us. Tolerance is for turning the other cheek to all the ways man wrongs God and forsakes religion, NOT for Christians to turn their backs on God.

We ignore and tolerate attacks on our religion on small and grand scales. When prayer was removed from schools, we were stymied into tolerance. When popular talk show hosts like *The View*'s Joy Behar says that things like "prayer is a substitute for logic," our tolerance silences us.

The deepest knife in the heart of Christian America came from our very own President, who dared mock religion and God like no other. When Obama accused the blue collar class of "clinging to their guns and religion," he was dismissing the nation's reliance and hope in God. Our

President put religion in the same category as voodoo or tarot reading when it came to hope. This left many Christian hearts weeping, but still tolerating the view that Christianity and God is weak. We did nothing.

Again our tolerance prevailed. No one answered that clinging to religion is precisely what we all need. In Obama's and the media's mind we should put our faith in the strength of man. This is not who we are. When we seek to put faith in God, we are mocked and insulted with implications of stupidity and bigotry. It was yet deeper than this. Their plan was to remove God entirely, to the point where they would take His place. We cannot condone this where our tolerance means silence.

When Obama and Congress are gone, Jesus will live on. God is the only constant entity in this world. To whom else shall we go? Our promise is in Him, and no one else. Keep clinging to Christ and believing that He can and He will!

> Crowns and thrones may perish, kingdoms rise and wane,
> but the church of Jesus constant will remain.
> Gates of hell can never 'gainst that church prevail;
> we have Christ's own promise, and that cannot fail.

False Premise 2: There is no Good vs. Evil

Make no mistake we are fighting a simple battle in this country of good versus evil. On a show in October 2010, Bill Maher talked with guest Richard Dawkins a hero and "respected" evolutionist and apparent atheist and asked, "How we could have the same brain?" "But how can some people and least 50% (actually it is more like 80%) of Americans who thinks the world was created by a man in the clouds, in six days who then needed to rest? I love that, he's so powerful, he can create the universe, but then he's pooped. (audience and panel support his with

167

raucous laughter). How can we have the same brain?" Dawkins responded quite frankly and without facetiousness, "I'm sorry to say, we don't. One of the main principles of Darwinian Theory was that there was brain variation – all the way from Einstein on the one hand to Sarah Palin on the other. "We are dumber country in this way," Bill Maher surmised.

America would have been nothing if not for God. God's laws and guiding principles for life is what has set us free. The founders paved the way for greatness in this country with God's hand and gave Him the glory. Faith and trust in God is what led this country to the greatness civilization on earth and He is what will allow us to get back there. It is not that we have been dumb. We have been blind, and only now are beginning to see.

False Premise 3: We are Strong Enough on Our Own

Apart from God, we can do nothing. All of the problems in our nation from our economy, failing schools, failing students, out of wedlock birth rates, and down to obesity require a return to Christ. On our own we cannot fix them no matter who is in Congress, in the Whitehouse, or chairman of the Federal Reserve.

All of these issues are a love issue. All of these issues are about desire. If we can redirect our desire for the Lord, we will be fulfilled. Psalm 81:10 says to us, "Open your mouth wide and I will fill it." There is nothing that God cannot do for us, or doesn't want to do for us. We just need to knock on the door and be ready to receive it. If we can desire to love him with our whole hearts, with faith in action, we cannot fail.

Because we have turned away from God's love, we have not known real love. Our love has been self-centered, which is the way to despair. We've over "loved ourselves with indulgences. We've engaged in "finding" ourselves, fixing ourselves, fixing each other, and comforting each

168

other with silly and spoiled notions that we are supposed to have it all. Truly, we have not loved ourselves; we've only been trying to make up the distance from God with worldly ideas of love. We cannot take this cheating heart any longer. Let's reform and get with the real program. Let's think of it as our very own two step recovery program: love God with all your heart and love your neighbor as you love yourself.

Most addiction recovery programs whether for drug addicts, alcoholics, or over eaters have a common element in their recovery program: reliance on God or a higher power to stay straight. We simply aren't strong enough to remain clean on our own. Our power alone cannot cast the demons of doubt, inadequacy, worry, and yearning out. We cannot be strong enough without God.

YES HE CAN!

It's time for us to take up our cross, let our yoke be with God and our burden light. We have to confront what is ailing us and heal the wounds with love, honor, and forgiveness. The values of Christ can strengthen our character and create a bond with our neighbors and our community. Let's get back to the basics of doing unto others as we would have them do onto us.

Taking up these crosses will not be easy. You think it's hard to turn away from that extra bite of pasta, not purchase that expensive pair of shoes you know you can't afford, or for a man to stop watching porn? Wait until you try to love your enemy. You've seen no willpower until you truly try and forgive trespasses. We know nothing of resistance until we try to halt our tongue from gossip and lashing out at someone who has wronged us. We need real love to see us through.

Worn and tired, blistered and bruised our souls seek rest and a peaceful place to dwell. For the last four years or so, we've had it out with the media, our Government and each other. Our nerves are fragile and hanging in the balance as we fret over finances, public education, joblessness, immigration, health care, impending socialism and war. Essentially, we are back to square one trying to figure everything out.

The last time we were worn out like this, Obama came in on his love and hope train and we felt rescued. We were not. The Tea Party now stands to try and rectify all of that and rescue us from plans put into place that distance ourselves from who we are as a nation. They are off to a good start, but alone are inefficient. Perhaps it's hokey to say, but I'll risk it. America is facing a love issue. I know this because what led us to Obama was that we loved him. We admired him. We were infatuated with how he made us feel about ourselves. Only it wasn't real love, because it was only about him. And as soon as he took his love away, we were diminished in his eyes and in many ways in our own.

The good news is that we don't belong to Obama. We belong to God. We were jolted awake by the Holy Spirit. Now we are to reckon with who we are, to whom we belong, and to take a stand for his Kingdom.

His love can take us higher if we let it. God's love and will for us runs deeper and holds unforeseen greatness for us individually and collectively. The even better news is that His love is unwavering and has been put to the test. It is there for us when, we fail, when we succeed, at our lowest and at our highest. No greater unconditional love exists; we only need faith and acceptance.

How can God's love rebuild a nation? One soul at a time. It's the army of one. My favorite quote about this comes from Paulo Coelho in *The Alchemist*. "…when we strive to become better than we are, everything around us becomes better too." We cannot do this without God's grace. The thing about becoming better is that you don't know if it's a mirage or if it's reality. Has anything really changed, or does it only seem so because your spirit is changed. Where before counting flaws and holding onto petty grievances and injustices led your course, you are now seeing the grace of God and receiving light of the world. Either way, doesn't matter, things are indeed better for you and indeed for the world now that you are in it.

More powerful than trying to tell us who we were, Obama showed us who we were not. It is in his rejection of us that we have found our true selves, aligned with our American exceptionalism, and embraced God as our King and our Creator. One of the best things to happen to us since Obama and our feelings of betrayal is that we have started over. Obama stripped us to the bones and made us face exactly who we are, were, and longing to be. In being remorseful about our unrequited love for Obama, we have started to look for love in the right places.

We have never loved America so much as we have today. We admire and revere her fortitude and her greatness. We marvel at how low she has been only to bounce back even higher than before. We learned about the Constitution beyond the first few and last couple lines we hear so much. Now, when we hear our national anthem, something about "land of the free and home of the brave" reverberates through our hearts and our souls calling us home. Inevitably, this home is in God.

God is indeed calling us home. We are at a crucial crossroads in our history. Our protesting and marches have taken us far and have served us well. It is a good start to elevate and support the conservative candidates and pray that they will win. This is a good start, but where do we go when the conservative fails or disappoints us. Because she will. She is only a human. He is only a man. A Republican majority, a Libertarian majority, a Democratic majority – all the same without a faithful Christian majority first.

Voting must not be about political party, rather voting values. Not the values of the candidate but our own. I am less concerned about who the candidates are than us striving to be better versions of ourselves. As we hold ourselves accountable, the more we expect or recognize those in others. It all works in tandem. We are each in our own recovery program. With each step we walk hand in hand with God to get us back to our greatness and on the path to goodwill. Yes, HE Can and Yes We Are.

God knows the corners of pride, lust, envy, jealousy, self-righteousness, and greed that haunt us. And He can fix them. He wants to fix them. Our game of hide and seek is over. We are so close to being found. We've been started on the right track. Don't stop moving towards the light now. We are almost home. We are found. Let's give ourselves over to the Lord and His amazing grace. Pray unceasingly. Give thanks and praise to the Lord. Show mercy to your neighbors and your enemies. Unburden your heart and mind in his comforting and living word. Lay your crosses down; rest your weary soul on his shoulders, and make a joyful shout unto the Lord. Hallelujah we are His! Thanks be to God forever and ever. Amen!

> Like a mighty army moves the church of God; brothers, we are treading where the saints have trod.
> We are not divided, all one body we,
> one in hope and doctrine, one in charity.
> Onward, Christian soldiers, marching as to war, with the cross of Jesus going on before.

ADDENDUM

We are saved by grace, not conservative values. God is not a conservative. He is not a liberal. His commandments, will, and laws are not about politics, not about us. God is love. His grace awakened me to my pride and arrogance. How easy it is to make God in my image instead of humbling myself to the truth that God's ways are not my ways, his thoughts are not my thoughts.

If you are anything like the old me--before these addendums and my run for Governor--attending rallies and supporting candidates roaring about the defending the constitution, protecting the unborn, securing the border, abiding by the constitution and protecting your rights as a US citizen, I urge you to deeply meditate on whether or not you have indeed (and wholeheartedly unbeknownst to yourself) made Government your God in a worse way than we've accused liberals of doing in their quest to give away tax dollars to welfare, schools, and government programs.

It's as true today as when I wrote this in 2011 that I fully believe Government cannot be our God. The irony that I missed then is that I had made Government a God. My role in influencing Government, my voice in supporting party politics, and my whole hearted belief that my party, my candidate was the right solution. All of these things were idols in my heart in mind that deluded me and others like me that my team needed to win to make the world a better place.

When I ran for Governor of Texas it's true I was already becoming disillusioned with politics and myself. Something wasn't adding up. I distrusted the party, myself, the system, and the process. Without stepping into the arena to challenge it and to be the change I wanted to see, I would have never seen so clearly how I'd made politics, government, a religion. And, how I used God to run from him.

I realized as I talked to people across Texas, observed so intimately week in and week out with all the other statewide candidates that all the energy and effort put into advancing a conservative agenda and conservative candidates, do very little if anything to advance God's agenda, or bring us all closer to him where we can freely accept and pour out his love, mercy and grace.

By invoking God into our discourse and talking so stridently against so many of his people, might we be distancing humanity from love, mercy, and grace. Could we be the reason struggling and broken people (just like us) turn away from God for fear that God might be like us, or heaven forbid agrees with us? Are we, our "values," a sizeable part of the problem, rather than the solution? Oh, how greatly humbled I was on that campaign.

Oh and this is why brothers and sisters, we must humble ourselves not only before God but before men. *"Let us accept gladly whatever can humble us before God and before men; this alone is the path to the glory of God."* Andrew Murray

I believe we are all being called to humility. Is it any wonder that Pope St. Francis is the Pope at this present hour? A beacon of humility and hope to the poor, offering words of absolution for all sinners. Hanging with the meek and the lowly and dressing down very much like Jesus did. Like Jesus he has confused many in the church refusing to admonish plainly gay marriage, rebuke abortion but instead speaking on love for all sinners.

"The first words uttered by Jesus in the New Testament were revolutionary, writes Peter Scazzero in *Emotionally Healthy Spirituality*: 'Blessed are the poor in spirit, for theirs is the kingdom of heaven.' The word he used described a beggar who had hit rock bottom, having been stripped of everything. Jesus was not describing a person in total destitution materially but one destitute of elevating themselves above others."

Finally this was an explanation of this beatitude that was crystal clear to me. The humility not to elevate myself above anyone else. This is the call of our time, for every one of us if we are going to have any chance of loving our neighbors as we love ourselves and love God with all our hearts and minds.

Remember Mel's diner—that sassy gum smacking waitress, Alice would ask, "What's the big idea? This is the BIG idea.

That we are all sinners, beggars. Even the best dressed, best educated, most prosperous of us are beggars, dependent on God to keep us breathing, keep the earth spinning, and calling us to rise each morning. Not one of us, not one, no matter how powerful or put together we seem can raise ourselves from the dead or know the hour God will stop the clock on our lives.

Peter Scazzero hits a homerun on this point in *Emotionally Healthy Spirituality.*

> Picture a beggar. Not someone you might find on the streets of a American city, looking for change to buy beer or cigarettes. I picture a person in such abject poverty that he is incapable of anything more than lying in a corner with a palm upraised, someone will take pity on him. Someone who knows he will die someone has mercy on him. Can you imagine that beggar say wasn't always like this; I graduated high school, I earn more th rest of these beggars; Look at what that other beggar on the co wearing. Doesn't he have any shame?"

We are this absurd sounding beggar and we don't realize it. We stand shoulder to shoulder as beggars to everyone else in this world. When we see that we will want to ease their pain and suffering, offering what little we can in our cup to put some in theirs, just as we rely on Jesus to do for us.

When I read the next excerpt, I read it thinking how does this person know me? I could have easily have written this but wouldn't have had the humility to the way this author did. I thank him for finding the words to this awareness in my old ways:

> We're each capable of turning what we see in the mirror int
> see this tendency clearly in myself when I believe I have .
> answers, not just for me but for those I judge as having mes
> and messed-up beliefs. "If only they knew what I know,
> would be so much better," I say to myself. I am comfortabl
> condescension because in the back of my mind, I think God
> my opinion. (And he has clout.) I'm just offering cl
> discernment because I am that close to the divine.

Jeff Cook, Seven

When Moses asked God who he should say sent him, God told Moses to say, "I AM." There's another famous "I am" response. The Times newspaper asked a number of intellectual authors to answer, "What's wrong with the world. Essayist G.K. Chesterson wrote, "I am."

Here I am, Lord. Have mercy on me, a sinner.

About the Author

Lisa has been a social and political activist for nearly 15 years. She is the author of the best-selling book, *Obama Tea Parties and God* and the e-book, *Politically Corrected*. Lisa was a talk-radio show host for over 12 years and a national radio and television commentator appearing regularly on Fox News Channel's "Glenn Beck," "Your World with Neil Cavuto," and Fox News 7. She has also appeared on MSNBC, CNN, BET, and Univision and has been featured and/or published in internet publications and newspapers such as *The Huffington Post, The Daily Beast, Breitbart, The Blaze, The Dallas Morning News, The Washington Times, The Austin American Statesman, World Net Daily* and many more. She has been a public speaker for more than 12 years speaking across the country to groups ranging from several thousand to intimate town halls.

In 2014, Lisa set out to bring a new face, message, and agenda to the Republican Party. She is the first African-American woman to run for Governor of Texas. With a focus on representing the underrepresented, the campaign addressed issues including: women's rights, dignity for immigrants, education reform, entrepreneurial access and opportunity for all Texans including the 18% of working Texans living in poverty. Though a first time candidate, Lisa gained national attention and raised consciousness across Texas and the country and received endorsements from BAMPAC, Central Texas Coalition for Life, and Texans United for Reform and Freedom. Defying the status quo, Lisa finished second against a highly funded establishment incumbent.

Lisa is a social and political strategist advocating for the underrepresented in work, life, and community. Lisa is the director of the PHENOMENALISM.org, a non-profit equipping women of color to lead in the 21st century and creator of *The Humility Project*, a blog navigating humility as the path to wholeness.

Other books by Lisa include *Politically Corrected* and coming soon, *The Freedom To Be The Angry Black Woman*.

www.lisafritsch.com
www.thehumilityproject.org
www.phenomenalism.org

www.ingramcontent.com/pod-product-compliance
Lightning Source LLC
Chambersburg PA
CBHW071353280526
45787CB00001B/304